IN MY
FATHER'S HOUSE

IN MY FATHER'S HOUSE

"THE KINGDOM OF HEAVEN IS AT HAND. MATT 4:17"

FAITH PARKER

TATE PUBLISHING
AND ENTERPRISES, LLC

In My Father's House
Copyright © 2016 by Faith Parker. All rights reserved.

No part of this publication may be reproduced, stored in a retrieval system or transmitted in any way by any means, electronic, mechanical, photocopy, recording or otherwise without the prior permission of the author except as provided by USA copyright law.

Scripture quotations marked (NASB) are taken from the *New American Standard Bible*®, Copyright © 1960, 1962, 1963, 1968, 1971, 1972, 1973, 1975, 1977, 1995 by The Lockman Foundation. Used by permission.

Scripture quotations marked (NIV) are taken from the *Holy Bible, New International Version*®, NIV®. Copyright © 1973, 1978, 1984 by Biblica, Inc.™ Used by permission of Zondervan. All rights reserved worldwide. www.zondervan.com

This book is designed to provide accurate and authoritative information with regard to the subject matter covered. This information is given with the understanding that neither the author nor Tate Publishing, LLC is engaged in rendering legal, professional advice. Since the details of your situation are fact dependent, you should additionally seek the services of a competent professional.

The opinions expressed by the author are not necessarily those of Tate Publishing, LLC.

Published by Tate Publishing & Enterprises, LLC
127 E. Trade Center Terrace | Mustang, Oklahoma 73064 USA
1.888.361.9473 | www.tatepublishing.com

Tate Publishing is committed to excellence in the publishing industry. The company reflects the philosophy established by the founders, based on Psalm 68:11,
"The Lord gave the word and great was the company of those who published it."

Book design copyright © 2016 by Tate Publishing, LLC. All rights reserved.
Cover design by Joshua Rafols
Interior design by Caypeeline Casas

Published in the United States of America

ISBN: 978-1-68319-331-9
1. Self-Help / Motivational & Inspirational
2. Religion / Christian Life / Inspirational
16.06.02

Contents

Foreword		7
1	Experiencing Life in My Father's House	11
2	A Vision Birthed	21
3	A Servant in the Father's House	27
4	Room in the Father's House	37
5	Peace in the Father's House	47
6	Celebration in the Father's House	57
7	Love in the Father's House	67
8	Intimacy in the Father's House	75
9	Joy in the Father's House	83
10	Instructions in the Father's House	91
11	Praise and Worship in the Father's House	99
12	Comfort in the Father's House	111
13	Security in the Father's House	125
14	Residency in the Father's House	133
Notes		145

Foreword

One of the most difficult issues for western Christians, especially in America is to read the word of God through the eyes of its intended audience – people in suffering. The Bible records countless passages directed to those who suffered for the faith to bring them encouragement and hope. Because life is so good for the western Christians it is very difficult to see the text in light of suffering. So when we read suffering we think of the suffering for living in a fallen world or possibly from the acts of sin we commit. But the believers of Haiti can see the words for what they really are – hope for the hopeless. Throughout In My Father's House, familiar passages of the Bible are given new life through illustrations of the truth displayed by impoverished believers. Time and time again we see with new eyes the words of the Bible coming alive in stories of God's miraculous actions. Over and over we are reminded of God's magnificent love for His people regardless of the conditions of their lives.

From beginning to end we are confronted with our willingness to substitute the material things of life for the Kingdom life . . . to see the first world lifestyle, full of its comforts and ease, as the life God desired for us. But in the words of these pages we see how deficient these things really are . . . how different the abundant life really is. And ultimately we are forced to examine how much we long for the power and presence of the Lord to be in our lives. The challenge for the reader is to do as Paul says in 2 Corinthians 13:5 "Test yourselves to see if you are in the faith; examine yourselves! Or do you not recognize this about yourselves that Jesus Christ is in you--unless indeed you fail the test?"

God proclaimed there was one man who was after His own heart, David. That man, David, confessed that there was only one thing he had asked of the Lord and would seek. "That I may dwell in house of the Lord all the days of my life." The Son of God, the Lord Jesus, even at the young age of twelve responded to His parents when they felt He had been lost to them, "Did you not know that I had to be in My Father's house?" What draws all faithful believers to desire more than anything else to be at home with their Heavenly Father? Is it the fallen world in which we currently live? Or is innate to desire and hope for something better? Is the longing for the life we were designed by God to live in a close relationship with Him? I choose to consider the last reason as the best. Man was created by God for an intimate relationship with Him, Even though man is marred by sin, the desire of every heart is intimacy with God.

Christ's message of "Repent for the Kingdom is at hand" is so enticing. Could it be that God's kingdom is here and available now? To the people of Jesus' day the coming Kingdom meant the Lord dwelling with His people. The coming of the Kingdom was the return of their true king and the life for which they had always dreamed. But in the days and years that followed that message, it was replaced with, "When we all get to Heaven." Heaven became the replacement for the Kingdom which Christ said was at hand. Few ever understood that Christ's words were literally true and that the Kingdom was available to mankind now. "Thy Kingdom come, Thy will be done right here on earth."

In her book Faith reveals the Kingdom here on earth to her readers through the most unlikely of places. Haiti is an island full of poverty, suffering, corruption, and desolation that its name is synonymous with all the plights of modern man. It is such a third-world place that there is no connection with us who live in the first world except through our financial aid and pity. Yet in the cultural darkness there is the shining light of the Kingdom brightly beating back the darkness of suffering and pain with a message of hope and victory.

Faith's vehicle is taken from the Lord's own words. "In my Father's house are many μονή" or places for dwelling or better seen in English as rooms. The rooms of the Father's house captures the essence of life in Christ through the lives of people who should have no reason to be hopeful. Firsthand accounts jump off the page with pictures of

Biblical truths about the abundant life that all believers should experience. Unfortunately few do. The reader is taken to places of great despair before being lifted to moments of mighty victory.

As a pastor for almost thirty years I can tell you that to have a member of the congregation serve with such great insight in their experiences is wonderful. But to have them put in written form those same insights and experiences shared with everyone to read and be inspired by is more than words can say. To see God work in the life of His believers in Haiti and the life of Faith Parker is a spiritually rich blessing that everyone should share.

Pastor Steve Clark
New Life Authentic Christian Community
Author of <u>The PLAN: Measureable Discipleship</u>

1

Experiencing Life in My Father's House

All of us had different experiences in the home in which we were raised. For some people, there are mainly fond memories, bad memories, or a mixture of feelings. There are also some of you that did not grow up in a place you can even call home. In the book I wrote, *Lost in the Wilderness*, I shared many experiences from life in my father's house. I lived in a home full of love with parents who were in love with the Lord. My father's love for his children was a picture or godly example of our Father God's love. Unfortunately far too many children grow up never seeing an example of a godly father at all. Their home life has no quality. They cannot imagine a quality life with the Heavenly Father.

If you grew up in an environment where you had a security and love from your parents, you may have had a similar experience to mine. Others may have moved from place to place, lived in the street, a foster home, or lived with friends or relatives. I was fortunate enough to grow up in a place I could call home. We did not move very often, but when we did, we still had a place that felt like home. My mother always kept the house clean and created a very comfortable environment. We always had furniture, chairs, sofas to sit on, table and chairs for dinner, and a comfortable bed in which to sleep. We always had heat in the winter and most of the time air-conditioning in the summer.

I was fortunate to have parents who were committed to being parents and caring for their children. I was able to grow up in a stable and secure environment. My mother never worked outside the home while I was growing up, but she was a servant within the house. She served her family in a passionate way while always making sure all our needs were met. She would cook three meals a day and prepare food for more than just the immediate family. She baked desserts and breads from scratch; did the laundry and hung the clothes outside to dry; ironed, sewed clothing, and much more without leaving any of our needs missed. The house was always spotless with no trace of seven children behind. Guests often commented that the house was clean enough to eat off the floors. She graciously served my father and all seven of her children for she delighted in supplying the needs of her family. My mother could stretch a dollar further than I have ever been able to do.

You may have lived in a small house or apartment without enough room for everyone who lived there. With five brothers and one sister, we always had plenty of room for everyone even if the size of the house was small. My brothers may not have felt the same way because three of them sometimes shared a bedroom. With only one sister, no matter what size our bedroom was, we always seemed to fit. Our family spent a lot of time together, crowding into the living room or sitting around a table in the eating area. It always felt cozy rather than crowded (with an exception of the times I wanted to be alone). In our house there was always room for one more whether it was at the dinner table, an overnight stay, or sometimes making room for a long-term guest.

Along with making room for everyone, life was peaceful in our house most of the time, but like any other family, it could get chaotic at times with nine of us. We had our typical sibling rivalry, times when we rebelled against parental authority and family feuds. You may have experienced living in a peaceful environment or you may have lived in an environment that had no peace at all. For some people, living at home is like going to war—you wake up to fighting and go to sleep with fighting. You wonder where your next meal will come from, how the next bill will be paid, or will your parents remain together. Peace in a home is vital to learning and developing. A child under stress does not perform well in school, begins to act out, and lives in fear from one moment to the next. We wonder why our teens and even preteens are carrying guns to school, cursing and being disobedient to authority, fighting in the streets, stealing, taking drugs, and drinking along with many other things. Do they experience peace in their homes?

If you were raised in or now live in a chaotic environment, it is hard to find restful peace. You are consistently pulled from one direction to another, and you feel you simply have nothing to be happy about or celebrate. The flipside to this is living in peace and celebrating every day of your life. In my father's house, we had many opportunities to celebrate throughout the year. We would celebrate nine birthdays, Christmas, New Years, Easter, Thanksgiving, my parent's anniversary, Valentine's Day along with other events. Sometimes we had parties and other times a big feast. Some celebrations were only for our family while others were shared with guests. Being the youngest of seven children, I had the opportunity to celebrate six weddings before my own. I could add all the times we celebrated various occasions at church. It felt like we just moved from one celebration to another, always looking forward to the next event.

A big celebration must have taken place in the heart of my mother and father the day I was born. They waited nine months for my arrival, hoping for a second little girl. It was long before ultrasound allowed parents to know in advance the sex of the child they were having. The anticipation just grew greater and greater as the weeks passed. There were already five boys in the family. My sister was now close to three years of age, and my parents wanted her to have a baby sister to love and grow up with. Excitement and an abundance of love flowed from their inner being on November 19, 1958, as the doctor announced the birth of a baby girl.

I understand my parents' feelings after giving birth to two daughters of my own. I remember looking at their tiny little bodies and loving them so much I just cried. These little babies were now dependent on me, and they needed my love to nourish them. My parents had enough love to go around to all seven of their children and an abundant amount of love left over to love others they came in contact with. My father had love for each and every member in the church in which he was the pastor, and if he moved to another church, there was enough love for all of those people as well.

Leaving none of his children without the warm feeling of love, there was intimacy in my father's house. He had a close personal relationship with each member of the family. We could be as close to him as we wanted because he never pushed us away. I had to make the personal choice just how intimate and close I wanted to be to my father. My father would give me a hug and kiss every morning before leaving for work and again before tucking me into bed for the night. I would often see my father hugging my mother, holding her hand or slipping her a kiss. I could sense a strong oneness between the two of them, a strength that would help them get through all the storms of life. They never stopped loving each other. Before his death, he proudly said that his love for my mother grew stronger and stronger every day. He knew from the day they were married and the two became one that he was devoted to her. My father's love for my mother derived from a close, long association with her and dedication of time spent with her. He had a detailed knowledge of my mother that could only have resulted from their intimate time together. If we want an intimate relationship with the Heavenly Father, we have to invest time with Him, be devoted to Him, and get to know Him.

Knowing my father loved me filled me with joy. It was a joy living in my father's house—just being in his presence. When I was young, of course, I did not look at things like I do now. You gain a lot of memories growing up, and then one day you muse over those memories. As an adult, I can now look back and see many things that were joyous experiences as a child. It was a joy to ride around town at Christmastime and look at all the lights and decorations, a joy to spend hours at the beach playing in the sand until you were sunburned. It was a joy to dress up and put on skits with my brothers and sisters for my parents. It was a joy that is unexplainable to be raised in Key West, Florida, and spend days out in the ocean diving and enjoying the underground wonders of the world. Almost every summer my father would take us to Six Flags Over Georgia and spend one or two days in the amusement park, riding roller coasters until I could hardly walk out of the park as they were shutting down. These are just a few of the many experiences that gave me joy while living in my father's house. Now I realize the greatest joy is realizing my father lived a life for Christ and set the example before me.

I do not want to leave you with the impression every part of life was joyous. Life in my father's house had many rules and instructions, and it was not a joy to follow all of the rules. We had a list of rules we all had to follow, or we had to suffer the consequences. Many times I remember asking the big question all kids ask, "Why?" Sometimes the only explanation I received was "because I said so" and other times I received the real explanation. I remember as a parent saying the same thing to my girls sometimes, and I bet there are many of you reading this book that said the same thing to your children. This answer is almost undeserving of respect. Children need instruction from their father so they grow up to understand the rules and their importance. Where would we be if the Bible had no instructions for living the way God intends for us to live? What if we had no rules or commands? Our society would be even more chaotic than it already is.

Even though I thought the rules were strict at times, I now know as an adult and parent the rules were for my own good and not nearly as strict as I thought they were at the time. The rules were for my own protection. By following my father's instructions, life was a whole lot smoother than if I had rejected his instructions. With my father's instructions, I was able to learn many important things necessary to live out my life successfully. I learned how to take care of myself, how to defend myself, how to ride a bicycle, how to drive a car, how to love, the importance of prayer and growing in the Lord, and how to be successful. I learned to manage money and so many other things. I could list pages of things I learned from my father's instructions.

If we followed our father's instructions, we were praised. If we disobeyed, we would be punished. When I made good grades in school, memorized my daily Bible verse, did my chores, sat still in church (and that was a big one when you are a preacher's kid on the front row every time the door opened), and graduated from high school or any action showing obedience to my father's instruction—I would be praised. They always wanted me to know they were proud of me and my accomplishments were pleasing to them.

In the evening we would have a family devotion time and worship God together. During these times we would come together as a family, sharing intimate time together and bond with each other and with the Lord. Sometimes we would sing praises to God, and we would always end our family devotion giving praise and thanks to God. One of the first simple prayers I remember saying children still learn today. Think about how many times God is being praised. "God is *Great*, God is *Good*, Let us *Thank Him* for our food. By His hands we all are fed, *Thank You Lord* for daily bread."

Think of a child's life for a minute. We should praise them from the minute they are born and throughout their life. We praise them when they hold their head up, when they roll over, when they can sit up by themselves, when they start to pull up on things, when they crawl, when they say their first word, when they take their first step, when they eat their spinach, and when they go to the potty and you finally get rid of those expensive nasty diapers. Parents praise children throughout school, sports, accomplishments, and you name it. The list is endless.

Praise supports comfort. Living in a comfortable home, sleeping on a comfortable bed, and having the perfect temperature in your home are all things that bring you comfort. Driving a luxury car or laying your head on a soft down feather pillow brings comfort to some people. Comfort can come from a warm hug, a gentle kiss, a big smile, or an encouraging word. Comfort is found in various ways in each individual. We all have our own love language, which when fed gives us comfort. You can all name specific items and actions comforting to you, but nothing compares to the comfort you can find in Christ Jesus.

Life in the homes of others could be very different than I experienced. In many homes, Satan is prevalent among the family. He is slyly moving around, causing confusion and dissention among the members. You may have someone in your home with an addiction to drugs, alcohol, or pornography. Life in some homes is an environment full of hatred, selfishness, bitterness, and physical or mental abuse. One of your parents may have abandoned the family so you were raised in a home with a single parent. Some of you have not been raised by either parent. Many grandparents are raising their grandchildren, or they are being passed off on someone else to look after. Many children grow up in an orphanage or foster parent homes. Then there are many children that have no home at all. They live in the street, or home may be called a car, a homeless shelter, or a cardboard box.

No matter what type of structure—do you live in a house that can weather the storms? Many people live in houses of wood, stone, brick, block, and other structures built by specifications of an engineer, but when the storms come, they still topple to the ground. A house can be built by the highest standards, but if the foundation is weak at any place, the entire structure will be affected.

Security systems are installed in a lot of homes for protection and are monitored twenty-four hours a day. Homes are prewired for wall-mounted, flat-screen televisions and built-in surround systems along with multiple other luxuries. We have many things in our homes to distract us and preoccupy our time so that Satan robs our homes. Yet he still runs free. If a tornado or hurricane hits, do you live in a house strong enough to stand or will it be destroyed and tossed about?

In the Heavenly Father's house, life is much better than in any family circumstance the world has to offer. Living in the Father's house, there are requirements to be met. We all need to be servants if we live in the Father's house. There is a job for everyone, and you must pitch in and do your part. There is room for as many as will come to live in comfort, experiencing joy, peace, and love in the Father's house. You will be able to experience the comfort of His loving arms wrapped around you and lifting you up when you live in His house. He will build an intimate relationship with each of His children and give them all the instructions they need to live a happy and successful life. Although He will praise you for your obedience—He is the Father that you should praise and worship every day of your life.

I find it amazing that people can describe life as they live it in their home just as I did throughout this chapter, yet describing living in His kingdom here and now seems so far out of reach and almost impossible for many to describe. We are so easily influenced by the world because it is visible that we overlook many of the principles of kingdom living since it is only obtained through faith. We approach kingdom living with only one foot in heaven while still leaving the other foot planted on earth. What would happen if we put both feet in the heavenly realm seeking first the kingdom of God and His righteousness? We just might become fully equipped with a kingdom heart and mind. Our complete lifestyle would then change, and people would notice you meant it when you prayed, "Your kingdom come. Your will be done on earth as it is in heaven."

Study Questions

1. Reflect on your family life for a few minutes. Did you feel secure in the home in which you were raised and/or do you feel secure in your current family environment?

2. Did you grow up in a home feeling loved? Is your current home filled with love?

3. Do you show love to the people living in your household?

4. Is your home a place of peace or constant turmoil?

5. Are there any changes you need to make to contribute to making your home more peaceful and secure? Do you need to make any changes to show love to others in your home?

2

A Vision Birthed

I had the opportunity to take a mission trip to Haiti. Although I was well aware of the poverty and economical situation in Haiti, I could not truly see the picture until I experienced it firsthand. My heart was broken and my spirit humbled even more from what I witnessed in Haiti. If you have a heart at all and go to Haiti, you will not return home the same. On this trip I encountered many experiences different from life back home in Hickory, North Carolina.

It all began on a brisk November morning in 2009 as I headed out for this mission trip to Haiti. I had looked forward to this trip for months. I had spent hours in prayer, studied the Bible, and sought the Lord for direction on this trip. One year earlier, the mission trip to Haiti had been planned. Upon arriving in Miami, Florida, flights into Port-au-Prince had been cancelled due to rioting in the town. My husband and I were shuffled out of the airport to spend the night in the closest motel to await a morning flight back home. A second attempt was successful, and we were on our way. During the flight, I spent time praying, reading my Bible, and listening to the voice of God. As I searched the Bible for encouragement, I started reading in Colossians 1. Paul is giving thanks for the faith in Christ Jesus and the love expressed to all the saints. He gives thanks for the Gospel being spread all over the world and for the fruit it bears along with growth within the church. Now I was headed to another part of the world to share the Gospel. My desire was to bear fruit as I shared the Gospel wherever I visited during this trip.

I got as far as verse 9, and I found my prayer for the week. I was never going to stop praying for the desire to be filled with the knowledge of His will in all wisdom and spiritual understanding that I may live a life worthy of the Lord and please Him in every way, bearing fruit in everything I did and growing in the knowledge of God. I wanted to be strengthened with "all might" according to his glorious power, unto all patience and longsuffering with joyfulness. If God would fill me with knowledge of His will and increase my wisdom and understanding during the week ahead, I could accomplish exactly what He had sent me there to do. I would plant seeds that would bear fruit in everything God would ask me to do, and I would do it with a joyful heart.

Within a few short hours, I found myself in the airport in Port-au-Prince, Haiti. It did not take long to find our luggage, get through customs, and head out the door to await our ride. Although it was evening, the temperature was high, and within minutes, sweat was running down my face. Haitians were hustling everywhere, and dozens of men would ask to carry your luggage hoping you would tip them. You could feel the poverty and see it in their faces as they begged for just one dollar. Where could you possibly start if you wanted to help the Haitians you laid eyes on? I would not have enough dollars in my pocket to even make a difference in the poverty I was seeing.

One of the members on our team arrived to tell us we would have to wait for a vehicle to arrive for us because the vehicle they were driving broke down on the way. Being informed to remain inside the fence for safety, I nervously waited and began to ask God for protection. What seemed like hours rather than a mere thirty minutes passed and in pulled our ride. An open back taxi pulled up (called a tap-tap) to take us to our destination. I wasn't sure if this one would get us to our destination before it broke down also. It was good to see the familiar face of another person on the mission team as we were introduced to the driver and our host for the week. Luggage was tossed in. I jumped inside while the men hopped in the back of this open vehicle, and we headed through downtown Port-au-Prince.

In My Father's House

The jagged roads jostled everyone as gas fumes took my breath. Cars honking horns, jetting in and out of lanes, missing us by a mere inch at times. We could see beggars in the street and prostitutes on the city street corner, toddlers and children walking the streets barefoot and many without clothes, trash everywhere, graffiti on every wall possible, and even naked adults running through the streets. Boisterous vendors were wedged into every square inch of space available on the streets, and many of the vehicles were intricately painted with a rainbow of colors. My heart was burdened. This country needed more than material things. They needed to be part of the family of God. After leaving the downtown area of Port-au-Prince, we headed a short distance out into neighborhoods. It became dark as we left the lights of the city to an area where there was only electricity for a few hours each day. The only light came from the headlights of the automobile and lights from lanterns in a few of the houses.

Haiti's history is marked with tragedy and oppression since winning freedom from French slavery and becoming the first independent black republic in the Western Hemisphere. The country has been plagued by dictators, extreme poverty, and devastating natural disasters. I could not imagine how a mere week spent there could possibly impact the widespread troubles. I had to remind myself every small step taken was leading toward success. If one good seed was planted in the ground, grew, and produced fruit, it could reap a tremendous harvest. God knows the plans He has for Haiti—plans to prosper and not harm the Haitians—plans to give them a hope and a future if they will trust in Him.[1] From the first night I arrived until the last minute of my stay, I could see a difference in the lives of Haitians living in the Father's house compared to those who did not. They had hope and a future—a future living in the Father's house for eternity.

Shortly after arriving and meeting the host family, I started to see a difference and continued to see this difference no matter where we went. Throughout the next ten days, I had the opportunity to gain a new perspective of what it is truly like to live in our Father's house. My heart was touched day after day as I saw the dedication of God's children whom I had the opportunity to work with. I have often heard the comment that people who have the least are more willing to share than those who have everything, and in Haiti, this was true. It was humbling just to be in the presence of such sharing and caring people.

I saw example after example throughout the week of what the Heavenly Father really wanted his children to look like. It was a picture I have personally not seen in any church I have attended. I had to evaluate myself and ask for forgiveness for not looking like I live in the Father's house. These Haitian Christians had taken possession of their inheritance and were leading a vibrant, victorious life like the Lord intended them to live. They were His children, and it showed. They accepted the abundant life Jesus came to earth to give. "I came that they may have life, and have it abundantly."[2] Even though they did not have many material possessions, they were living an abundant life. The children of God did not worry what tomorrow would bring because they had an understanding of the spiritual riches they had already obtained.

God's plan for a family is a place of love, joy, peace, and discipline along with many of the same things we experience in the family of God. The family unit is meant to be a blessing to the world, and it is falling short. Satan is trying to tear apart the family because he hates it with a passion, and he is trying to do the same with the family of God. Families are being shredded apart by the enemy leaving many people with devastated lives in the church as well as out of the church. It is time Christians move forward with all God has planned for them in their personal family life and in family life within the church.

You must put God first. Matthew 6:24, "No one can serve two masters; for either he will hate the one and love the other, or he will be devoted to one and despise the other."[3] God must be first above all else if we are His children. We must recognize we are not all we should be—that God has even greater things for us. Paul writes in Philippians 3:13–14,

> I do not regard myself as having laid hold of it yet; but one thing I do: forgetting what lies behind and reaching forward to what lies ahead, I press on toward the goal for the prize of the upward call of God in Christ Jesus.⁴

You must continually reach toward your goal of godly success laying up your eternal prize in the Father's house. Philippians 1:20 says,

> Live according to your most earnest expectation and hope so you will not be put to shame in anything, but that with all boldness, Christ will even now, as always, be exalted in your body.⁵

As you experience some of the blessings you receive in the Father's house, I hope you are committed to change and act like a child living in His house. I hope you become a child with inner peace, exuberant joy, an abundance of love, and a willingness to be His servant. I hope you will strive for a more intimate relationship with the Father and allow Him to instruct your every move. Then at the beginning of every day and at the end of every evening, you can praise and worship the Father.

Study Questions

1. Is Christ the head of your home?

2. Do the people living in your home see Christ in you?

3. Are you serving the one and only Master: the Lord Jesus Christ?

4. Do you invest time in getting to know your Heavenly Father, talking to Him in prayer, reading the Word of God?

5. Are you willing to serve God wherever He wants to send you, or do you put limitations on what you are willing to do? Would you avoid running away from God's will regardless of the cost?

6. Do you see the significance you can make in the lives of others?

3

A Servant in the Father's House

We arrived at the church where we would be holding meetings for the first few days. The first service was going on in the church so we went to the basement area where the bishop and his wife lived in their home. All seven people working on the team for the week had safely arrived to where we would stay for the first few days. It did not take long to start feeling the dedication to service flowing out of the host family. They welcomed you into their home as if it was your own. They carried our luggage from the car, took it to the room in which we would be sleeping, and then as the revival meeting was coming to an end, we were hustled into the church to be introduced to the local church members. The warmth of love and acceptance made me feel more like royalty than just a common American.

As soon as everyone was gone from the church, we sat at the table for a meal the women had prepared. The only light we had was an oil lantern or the flashlights we brought from home. They were thrilled we had come to work for the Lord in their country, and they obviously planned to serve you while you were there. I felt loved and appreciated from the very first moment I arrived. I received warm hugs as if we had been friends for a long time. We were family although we had never met each other. It was like getting together for a reunion and meeting family for the first time.

When we prepared to retire for the evening, I realized the owners of the home gave up all beds including their own for the team of missionaries to have a place to sleep. I watched them prepare a place to sleep on the hard concrete floor, and I felt bad for taking the bed.

Here I was in a country with so little—a place where the majority do not even have a bed to sleep on. I thought to myself—this is something you seldom see back home. When we have guests, we usually put them in a guest room or one of our children's bedrooms but rarely give up our own comfort to comfort others.

They actually took their wooden dining room furniture outside the house and placed it under a sheet of plastic to make room for people to sleep. Could you imagine taking your dining room table outside in the weather and leaving it for ten days to accommodate a guest? I don't think so. We would be too proud for our neighbors to see it in our front yard and certainly would not want to see it ruined by the weather. Although they tried to protect what the Lord had provided for them, it was just "stuff," and people were more important.

The food preparation for just seven of us kept three women cooking all day to prepare two meals. Everything prepared was fresh from the garden. Every herb and spice used was hand ground or chopped piece by piece before starting to prepare the meal. If they did not have something they needed, one woman would start walking to the market a mile or more away and return with it an hour later. It was an all-day job preparing what looked like a feast rather than preparing their typical meal consisting of black beans and rice. Some of the food was prepared outside on a small coal bed, brought into the house, and finished in the gas oven. As much as they were able, they cooked outside to avoid adding to the already ninety plus degree temperatures inside the home.

When preparing chicken, they did not remove it from a grocery store package ready to start cooking. Instead the women had a fresh chicken they still had to clean from the beginning before they could prepare it. This was no simple five-minute task. Then when it was time to sit down and eat, you were given a chair and served on their few glass pieces of dinnerware. We could see them sitting on anything available—eating from a metal bowl or plastic container. This was quite a humbling experience. I hated to even eat the food knowing they have so little and had worked so hard to prepare it just to watch it vanish in minutes. I was informed they purchased extra items they rarely get for themselves to eat. I wanted them to sit down and enjoy the food themselves. I was abundantly blessed at home with food, and I just wanted to see them enjoy the extra for themselves.

Read the words Jesus spoke in the Gospel of Luke 17.[1] I simply put this situation in its place. Suppose one of us had a servant cooking and cleaning, looking after the missionaries' needs all day long. Would you say to the servant when she completes the day's chores and cooking, come along now and sit down to eat? Or would we rather say cook some more and wait on me hand and foot while I eat and drink, then you may eat and drink. Would you thank the servant for doing all they were asked to do? When I thanked these women, they merely let me know it was their duty. They humbled themselves not wanting any great recognition.

This is real service in the Father's house. When you do all you are told to do and listen to the voice of God, you should say, "I am an unworthy servant, having only done my duty." If you live in the Father's house, you have an obligation to be obedient to the Father and be His employee with no concern as to how you will be paid or how much the pay will be, for you will have great rewards in heaven.

When it was time to take a bath in the evening, the women carried five gallon buckets of water to their shower stall since there was no running water. They treat the water with a Clorox solution to make sure you have clean and sanitized water rather than using the polluted water they generally bathe with. Not only would we not go to all this trouble to see our guest get a clean bath, we would be more concerned about being clean ourselves. We would probably bathe first and let them have the hot water left over or wait until our hot water heater replenished itself.

They were true servants of God serving His servants. It was like Paul described in Philippians when he said our attitude should be the same as that of Christ Jesus.[2] Paul tells us Jesus took on the very nature of God, made Himself nothing and became a servant. The ladies serving us emptied themselves, dropped their own desires for days, and became servants. They went out of their way to make us as comfortable as possible and tried to keep us from getting sick. Paul goes on to say in verse 7–9 that when Jesus humbled Himself and became obedient to death, even death on the cross, God exalted Him to the highest places. If you have this Christ-like attitude and humble yourself to serve others, do you not think God will exalt you as well?

Our host would rise first in the morning and retire last at night and never stopped working in between. They served wholeheartedly as if they were serving the Lord and not man.[3] Servants in the Father's house do not have divided service. They knew they were serving only one master, and they were devoted to Him. These women were serving the Lord with gladness by serving His servants. They took great delight in making sure we were provided for and the food was prepared with bottled water to avoid any sickness.

Once we left Port-au-Prince and went into the mountain areas, the servants worked even harder. To prepare a meal, they had to cut down a tree, cut up the wood, and feed sticks into the fire under a pot resting on three rocks. To make matters worse, they did this cooking in a shed with only a door for ventilation in the heat of the day. They worked under these conditions from 6:00 a.m. to 3–4:00 p.m. until they finished the late afternoon meal that was lunch and dinner combined. To get water, they send five or more women down a steep hill approximately one mile to the water supply trickling out of the mountain, waiting until they filled a five-gallon bucket to place on their heads. With water sloshing from the buckets as they walked the slippery wet trail, they started the one-mile hike back up the hill. The path was very rocky and rutted out. I made the trip once without a bucket, and I was totally exhausted when I reached the top, and I was in pretty good shape. The heat alone would zap out all of your energy. My clothes were soaked by the time I reached the top of the hill without a sloshing bucket of water. They would take trip after trip until they filled a fifty-five-gallon drum every day for us to bathe, to do laundry, and for washing the dishes.

A single mother hosted the home where we stayed in Belami. She had two daughters and a son. Her husband had been killed a few years earlier in an automobile accident while in the United States picking up supplies to take back and sell at the local market. She was a beautiful lady with a humble spirit, but now she was left to take care of the family on her own. The love of Christ just poured out of her innermost being. Although she did not have many worldly possessions, she was willing to freely share and give up what she did have. Her children were just as sweet. You would see them lending a hand and doing whatever necessary to assist their mother in getting the daily chores completed. I thought of the laziness of our teenagers here in the United States as I watched her teenage daughters sweeping the dirt lawn to get up all the lose dirt. Our teenagers have lawnmowers, many in which all they have to do is ride them around, yet they do not even want to mow the lawn. Their mother loved and reached out to everyone in the community, and everyone had to have seen a glimpse of Jesus in her life. She worked and served from daylight until dark day after day.

When it came time to sleep, the arrangements now left her family and the Haitians who came with us from the city on a straw mats in the outdoor kitchen, on the rocky ground, or on the concrete front porch. Neighbors would bring fresh things from their gardens to share even though they did not have enough for their own family. If they had a few ripe bananas, they would bring some to share. The Haitian rule was great: "You never eat alone." If an adult or even a child had something to eat, they shared it with everyone around them. Once I witnessed five children sharing one small cracker. They would each take a tiny nibble and pass it on to the next child in the group. They did not want to see the person beside them go hungry if it only meant having one bite of food. For us, a Ritz cracker is only one bite in the beginning.

Seeing these village children share the food like they did, my thoughts went straight to the story in John 6 when Jesus fed five thousand people. Jesus did not want to see any of them go away hungry. Even though He asked Philip in verse 5, "Where are we to buy bread, so that these may eat?"[4] this was merely a question to test Philip. Jesus already knew what He was going to do. Andrew, Simon Peter's brother, exclaimed that there was a lad close by that had five barley loaves and two fish. Can you imagine the faith it must have taken for the disciples to invite five thousand people for dinner and have them sit down knowing there was so little food? The story goes on to tell how Jesus took the loaves and the fish, gave thanks, had the food distributed, and all the people had as much as they wanted. They even gathered twelve baskets of leftovers. Oh how I wish I could say the people in this area of Haiti had enough food to go around and even leftovers to gather. I once witnessed a mother mixing dirt with the food so it would go further and fill her children's stomachs. We cringe when our kids get dirt near their mouths.

These small children that shared what little food was given to them had enough faith to believe if they shared what little they had, they could prevent the whole group from going hungry. They did not worry where the next bite would come from. They merely shared what they had at the moment. How much faith would you have if you were in this same situation—if you had one cracker and four hungry friends standing around you? Could you take just one nibble and pass the cracker on to the next person? Or better yet, could you just give it away? Could you truly serve others and not think about eating the whole cracker knowing you were hungry yourself? Nowhere else in the world are there so many overweight people as there are in America, and yet starving people are all around us. Be generous and do not miss out on a blessing. Proverbs 22:9 says, "He who is generous will be blessed, for he gives some of his food to the poor."[5]

Think of the story of the rich young ruler in Matthew 19. He came to Jesus and asked Him what good thing he could do to obtain eternal life. I think Jesus must have been highly insulted with the question because He replied, "There is *only one* who is good." Then Jesus instructed the young ruler to keep the commandments if he wanted to obtain eternal life. The ruler asked which commandments

Jesus wanted Him to obey. Oddly enough, I am sure many people today ask which commandments they are to obey like maybe they can leave one or two out so the commandments conform to their own lives rather than making changes in their lives. Then Jesus tells him not to murder, not to steal, not to commit adultery, not to give false testimony, to honor his father and mother, and to love his neighbor in the same manner in which he loves himself. It is a pretty tough package, but the rich young ruler simply tells Jesus he has done all these things.

Then the ruler wants to know what he is still lacking. Oh how you and I need to continuously come to Jesus and ask this same question, "What am I still lacking?" But what if Jesus then asked you to do the same thing He asked of the rich young ruler? What if to be made complete you were asked to go and sell all your possessions and give to the poor? Would you do it or merely walk away like the young ruler did, grieving over this tough order? When you see how someone with almost nothing is willing to share like believers in Haiti, I caught a glimpse of just how hard it will be for a rich man to enter the kingdom of heaven like Jesus said. Knowing Christ Jesus is a lot easier than being a true follower of Jesus. If the young rich ruler wanted to be a follower, it would come with a cost so he merely walked away. What would you do?

Most people have no idea what it is really like to be a servant. Being a servant in the United States is a whole lot easier and a whole lot more comfortable. From what I witnessed, the Haitian definition of a servant had a deeper meaning than the definition in the American dictionary. To most people, a servant is a person paid to wait on others and do work in their house. A servant is someone to boss around and give orders. In Matthew, Jesus said, "And whoever wishes to be first among you shall be your slave; just as the Son of Man did not come to be served, but to serve, and to give His life a ransom for many."[6]

In the Father's house, a servant is someone who serves to meet the needs of others and puts others ahead of themselves. They have the occupation of being a servant by choice. Generally, there is no monetary pay, but the rewards and blessings are of great value. Servants care about others from the heart and don't need orders from anyone to get the job done. They see the need and get to work.

Samuel was a good example. He was a servant, and he listened. Dedicated to the Lord, Samuel served in the house of the Lord as a young boy. While Samuel was lying down in the temple, the Lord called Samuel three times. Thinking it was Eli calling, Samuel went to him in the night to see what he wanted and was sent back to lie down twice. Once Eli realized the Lord was calling Samuel, he told him what to say next time he was spoken to. In verse 10, Samuel says, "Speak, Lord, for Your servant is listening."[7] After personally seeing the nature of servants in Haiti—I merely had to say, "Speak Lord, for *Your* [referring to me] servant is listening." I knew a greater meaning of being a servant in the house of the Lord. I had a clearer picture of what being a servant in the Father's house was supposed to look like. I had to follow the instructions Samuel gave his people when he told his people, "Do not fear, do not turn aside from following the Lord, but serve the Lord with all your heart."[8] To be a committed servant, you cannot turn aside. You must remain a committed servant, and the Lord will not abandon you.

There is a verse found in Joshua 24 which says, If it is disagreeable in your sight to serve the Lord, choose for yourselves today whom you will serve: whether the gods which your fathers served which were beyond the River, or the gods of the Amorites in whose land you are living; but as for me and my house, we will serve the Lord."[9] The latter part of this verse is familiar to most Christians. We even sing a song that says, "As for me and my house we will serve the Lord…Yes we will serve the Lord." We read this verse (even believe this verse), recite the verse, and hang the verse on our walls. Yet we take the commitment so lightly. In the same way, Joshua told the children of Israel to choose for themselves whom they will serve. You have to choose whom you are going to serve. The choice is up to you.

In the world in which we live, there are many things tugging at us and dragging us in many directions. These things influence our decision as to whether we will serve God or not. The world tries to entice you into serving many things other than God. You fight against your own flesh that wants you to do things that are wrong. We live from one temptation to another. It is up to us to choose to remain faithful to God and not give in to fleshly desires. The fact is the devil is trying to make choices for us as well. I have heard many people refer to temptation as being from God. In the book of James, chapter 1, James warns us not to blame it on God when we are tempted. He adamantly says that God is not tempted by evil and He does not tempt anyone. So you must realize where temptation comes from and not give in to the temptation. If you are tempted and carried away by your lust, it will give birth to sin. Next you will give into the lust, and the sin is accomplished. Then look at the consequences. It brings forth death.[10]

If you have not made the choice to serve the Lord, don't wait another moment. Once you make the choice to serve God with all your heart, soul, and mind, you will want to serve others. It will come naturally because you desire to look like Jesus. Let your response be like that of the children of Israel. "Yes, I will serve the Lord." Accept all the conditions that come along with being a servant of the Lord and get with it! Make a conscious decision to serve the Lord the rest of your life and put your trust in Him.

Study Questions

1. Have you ever wondered what difference your serving the church makes?

2. Would you be missed if you stopped serving or is your service so slight you would go unnoticed?

3. If everyone serves to the same degree you serve, what would our churches across America look like? Would it be a healthy, growing, nurturing environment full of acts of service?

4. Examine yourself and see how you are truly serving in the Father's house. Are you doing your part to serve?

5. Can you identify the area of service that you effectively contribute to the body in which you are a part? It only takes one person not doing his part to make the body dysfunctional or not functional to its full potential.

6. Have you made the commitment, "As for me and my house we will serve the Lord"?

4

Room in the Father's House

After the third day, we packed up and headed to the country. We were going to have revival in a small area called Belami, a mountainous region of Haiti. On the journey to Belami, the ladies rode with the bishop in his automobile while all the men jumped aboard a tap-tap (Haitian bus). Knowing the vehicle was just repaired from the breakdown coming to the airport, I was slightly reluctant about climbing in the vehicle. I wondered if the vehicle would not make the journey. The trip should take approximately six hours with most of the travel being on dirt roads through the country. Before leaving, it was brought to our attention the tires were really worn out, and we wondered if they would make the trip. But as the Haitians say, "No problem." So we jumped in and off we went. It is only no problem until you have a flat tire because there is no spare tire. Being fortunate enough to have four tires on the car, a Haitian could not expect to find enough money to have a fifth tire just in case it was needed.

Approximately one hour into the trip, you guessed it—flat tire! Luckily our driver was able to slowly creep to the next tire repair stand. You would see tire repair stands every few miles along the way, and now I know why. In this poverty-stricken country, people cannot afford to replace them so they repair them over and over again until there is no rubber left to repair. After a thirty-minute repair in the scorching heat, we were back on the road for the duration of the trip.

We had been riding for hours on rough, rutted roads, crossing rivers and bouncing in the vehicle so much my body felt bruised by the time we arrived in the evening. As we came to the area where the voodoo temple was located, the driver informed us to pray the vehicle did not break down in this town because it could be very dangerous. So we all began to pray, asking the Lord to keep us safe and deliver us through this region of danger. God answered our prayer, and the journey continued in safety.

For the first few hours, the limestone roads were very dry and dust was blowing everywhere. Of course, there was no air-conditioning in the vehicle, so it was coming into the windows. To avoid getting motion sickness, I hung my head out the window and inhaled even more dust. My hair turned white and stiff from the limestone dust, and I could rub it off my face. It was after this event I was informed it would be best if I wore a paper mask over my face and a scarf on my head. Guess that answered the question in my mind as to why the Haitian women had scarves over their hair when we got into the vehicle. I will know next time!

The roads twisted and turned around the mountains. I thought we would never arrive at our destination. As we approached the last five-mile stretch, it started to rain, and the roads became very slippery. Now you can imagine what happens when you already have slick tires. The packed wet limestone became like slippery clay in the hands of a potter sitting at his wheel, and that is exactly what happened to the man behind the wheel of this automobile. This caused the vehicle to start sliding as we went up the hills. We approached several hills where we had to walk to the top and let the driver get local people to help push the vehicle to the top as it slid all over the road. One hill too many and far too steep—we were told we would have to walk the rest of the way to where we would be staying.

Grabbing bottles of water for the journey, four of us ladies headed toward the village in Belami. It was all uphill from there, and I had no idea how far. In the hot, humid temperatures, we began the journey I thought would never end. With every mountain we climbed, I was told it was just over the next mountain. I started singing a song that I learned when I was a kid, "She climbed another mountain, she climbed another mountain...and what do you think she saw?

She saw another mountain." For quite some time, another mountain without a house in sight was all I saw. The road was steep, and the heat was so intense with very little shade to stop and rest in. There was no place to sit down unless you sat on the wet dirty road.

We walked for over an hour, stopping to rest along the way. Finally I could see a house around the next bend in the road. As we approached the little village, I sensed eyes watching us as we walked closer and closer to our destination. Children were coming out to the road to see who was coming into town. Peeping around trees and standing on the edge of the road, you could tell the children were not used to seeing visitors in the area. It was a delightful sight for them to have a visitor in the area because they knew they were mostly missionaries who were coming to help them out.

When Jesus entered Jericho, a wealthy tax collector named Zacchaeus wanted to see who Jesus was. He was a short man so he could not see over the large crowd. He ran ahead of Jesus and climbed into a sycamore tree hoping to see Him as He passed through. When Jesus reached him, He looked up and told Zacchaeus to come down because He was going to stay at his house today. At once he came down and gladly welcomed Jesus. People in the crowd started to mutter and could not understand why Jesus was going to be the guest of a sinner. Zacchaeus spoke to the Lord and was ready to give to the poor and repay those whom he had cheated. He was saved that day because the Son of Man came to seek and to save what was lost.[1]

Unable to speak their language, we smiled and waved at the children, and they started to come out from behind the trees. The children followed us along the trail. They were chattering and curious about where we were headed. None of the children were clean, and many of the younger ones were without clothes. These poor and often homeless children knew a group of missionaries were coming into the area. We were coming to be their guests for the week. They were curious. They wanted just a glimpse, and they hoped we had brought something for them—maybe a garment to wear, a bite of food for their hungry stomachs, a hug from warm loving arms, or maybe someone would simply say, "I love you, and I am coming to your house to see you today." They were looking for something refreshing, for a glimmer of hope, or for an opportunity of something better. Here we were going into this village to share Jesus with the lost. Would people be saved this week? Would people turn from their sinful ways and believe in Jesus Christ? Would they get so excited about Jesus they would run to the church to get a glimpse of Jesus? Would they want to know whom Jesus is like?

We passed several houses, a local school, and then we saw the house where we would be staying. Upon arrival, we were told that our bags would arrive later. They sent young men down the mountain to get our luggage and carry it up on foot. Hours later, our luggage did arrive on the heads of these young men. Our husbands (sent by bus) were to arrive soon. Hours passed and then there was deep darkness. With no electricity, sitting there in the dark, I was anxiously waiting to see my husband arrive through the woods. Then voices speaking English were heard in the distance, and the men had arrived. They too had to walk the last several miles up goat trails from where they had been dropped off to get to the place where we would work the next five days. It did not take anyone long to retire for the evening since we were all exhausted from the long day of travel.

The house was very small with only two very small bedrooms. My room had one bed and two cots for four of us to sleep. There was barely enough room to walk around. Luggage was stacked on the floor until you needed something. Another couple was in the other bedroom. The bishop and his wife along with one more person on the team camped out in the small living area of the home. This entire house could have fit into my living room back home, but yet there was enough room for everyone.

The next morning after a cup of instant coffee we brought from home, we decided to take a hike up to the church site. We were taken to the top of the mountain where their local church was under construction. A very narrow, rutted road widened just enough to get a vehicle through with supplies for the construction. The building site where the church was under construction had previously been the site used by the voodoo priest. There was a large tree on the top of the mountain where they practiced satanic worship. Years ago on a previous mission trip, several went to this site praying for the Lord's provision on the purchase of this site for a church. They claimed the property for the Lord and had hopes of building a church in the near future so the people in the area had a place to worship God.

The Lord provided, and a few years later, they were able to purchase the mountaintop land. With only a goat trail leading to the top, it was necessary to open up a road to get trucks in with building materials. The locals set out to accomplish this task, and at the end of one week, a single-lane road was prepared for approximately one-third mile. Some areas were dug up to six feet deep in the mountain. Many trees were cut down by hand. What they dug from one area would be hauled by wheelbarrow to other areas to build up the road. It was a task in the United States that would only be completed with chainsaws, bulldozers, front-end loaders, and other pieces of equipment. People in the area were excited about the new church and worked hard to do their part. Adults and children all contributed to the hard labor in getting the site prepared. They wanted a place with plenty of room to come together and worship the Lord.

It was a beautiful site with a 360-degree breathtaking view. From this site you could see mountains, valleys, rivers, and the ocean all at once. The mountainsides were covered in palm trees, banana trees, and other tropical trees. I had visited many Caribbean islands. The view from this mountain was as lovely as any I had seen. On the mountaintop stood three concrete block walls of the future church building. There was no roof, no floor, no doors, and no windows installed. The local men constructed handmade benches out of wood so they could begin to worship within the walls. There was no pastor for the church, but they had a local teacher who was gifted in teaching the word of God. They were already meeting on a weekly basis.

On the first night of revival, I was amazed at what I witnessed taking place. As I arrived, men were taking the cement blocks located on site for construction, stacking them up and putting planks of rough wood across them to make more benches for people to sit on. There must have already been twenty benches approximately fifteen feet long with ten on each side of the building. I did not see that many houses or people anywhere. I could not imagine why they would need to make more benches. There were only about fifteen people there at the time the service was to start.

These few Haitians started singing in Creole, and one by one people started drifting into the building. Then five to ten came at a time. The front benches started filling up with children from one year of age and up. Bench after bench would be filled as deacons led the people to their seats. They strategically seated the people filling the benches from the front to the back. Soon all the benches were filled with people, and they started seating them on the planks. Before long, all the planks were filled, and people were standing in the back doorway. Then children would start to pick up the toddlers and hold them on their laps to make room for more children in the front rows. People stood on the foundation of the unfinished wall, hung in the windows, and packed in every doorway. There was room in the Father's house for all who came. There were over five hundred people every night for four nights packed into the Father's house. Curious as to where all these people came from, I asked the question. They had walked miles and miles to come to the Father's house down dark trails with no flashlights. They just followed the light powered by a generator on the top of the mountain. They longed to be with the Father in His house.

What a beautiful picture of the story of the birth of Jesus is told in Luke 2:8–20:

> There were sheepherders camping in the neighborhood. They had set night watches over their sheep. Suddenly, God's angel stood among them and God's glory blazed around them. They were terrified. The angel said, "Don't be afraid. I'm here to announce a great and joyful event that is meant for everybody, worldwide: A Savior has just been born in David's town, a Savior who is Messiah and Master. This is what you're to

look for: a baby wrapped in a blanket and lying in a manger." At once the angel was joined by a huge angelic choir singing God's praises: Glory to God in the heavenly heights, Peace to all men and women on earth who please him. As the angel choir withdrew into heaven, the sheepherders talked it over. "Let's get over to Bethlehem as fast as we can and see for ourselves what God has revealed to us." They left, running, and found Mary and Joseph, and the baby lying in the manger. Seeing made them believe. They told everyone they met what the angels had said about this child. All who heard the sheepherders were impressed. Mary kept all these things to herself, holding them dear, deep within her. The sheepherders returned and let loose, glorifying and praising God for everything they had heard and seen. It turned out exactly the way they'd been told!"[2]

Here we were on the top of the mountain. Bright lights come on from the generator, and the Haitians may have thought they were settled down for the evening. Then as the voices started praising God, it was like an angelic choir. People were drawn to see for themselves what was happening on top of the mountain at the church site. They dropped everything they were doing and ran down the trails. They wanted to come into the Father's house and worship and praise God and hear what was going to be said. They must have stopped along the way or shouted out to their neighbors, "Come! There is singing on the mountaintop." Even those who did not believe in Jesus came along out of curiosity. When they arrived, they saw the American team of missionaries, heard the angelic voices singing praises to God, listened to the band (generator-powered), and just had to take a seat.

Sitting in my chair with tears streaming down my cheeks, I thought why this scene could not happen in America? I was like one of the sheepherders. I just let loose and cried, glorifying and praising God for everything I had seen and heard. This too had turned out exactly the way I had been told by those who had come and experienced this before me.

Why do people find it so hard to come to the Father's house? We have cars with heat in the winter and air-conditioning in the summer. We still do not want to come out in the rain or extreme cold. The Haitians would hike up and down rocky trails in the dark with extremely hot temperatures, arriving soaking wet with sweat to be in the Father's house. I will always cherish these thoughts and hold them deep within my heart.

We must love our Heavenly Father so much that we long to come into His house and be in His presence. There is room in the Father's house for all who will come.

> In my Father's house are many dwelling places; if it were not so I would have told you; for I go to prepare a place for you. If I go and prepare a place for you, I will come again and receive you to Myself, that where I am, there you may be also.[3]

The Father will prepare enough room for all who want to come. When it is time, He will come back to get us and take us home. The Father has constructed room after room and created enough space for all His children to come home. He will come to get us when everything is ready. Jesus said, "I will not leave you as orphans; I will come to you."[4] We are a real family in the house of the Father.

The Christians in Haiti eagerly await heaven. For they know their citizenship is in heaven, from which they eagerly wait for a Savior, the Lord Jesus Christ.[5] They are anxious to go home and be with the Father. They know it is a better life and a better home. They certainly have not stored up treasures for themselves on earth where moths and rust destroy and where thieves break in and steal. They are storing up for themselves treasures in heaven where nothing can destroy and no one can steal. Their heart is where their treasure is, and it is in the Father's house.[6]

They look forward to the heavenly home—the final dwelling place for the saints. They do not worry if their earthly tent is destroyed. While they work hard to build the church for a place to worship now, they are fully aware they have a building from God, an eternal house in heaven, not built by human hands.[7] They know they are fellow citizens with God's people and members of God's household. They looked forward to their inheritance like Abraham did. They were looking forward to the city with foundations, whose architect and builder was God. Abraham did it by keeping his eye on an unseen city with real, eternal foundations—the city designed and built by God.[8]

In God's house, there is room for all who will come. There is an open invitation, and we simply need to RSVP: "I am coming!"

Study Questions

1. Living in the Father's house requires a willing heart and a lot of sacrifice. Are you willing to give up your comfort to live in the comforting arms of the Father in His house?

2. Living in the father's house takes a lot of dedication? Just how dedicated are you to being part of the family and making room in your life for whatever God wants from you?

3. How solid is your foundation? If the storms come, will you be able to stand because your house is built on the Solid Rock or are you built on shifting sand?

4. Can you truthfully say you are ready and eagerly awaiting Christ to return and take you home to an eternity with Him in His house?

5

Peace in the Father's House

The Christian Haitians I met have peace living in the Father's house. As I watched the faces of the children of God versus the nonbelievers, I could see they had peace even though they were living in such a poor, rough, and unsanitary environment. They simply trust the Lord to protect them and take care of their needs. They do without so many things we take for granted every day. Without peace from the Heavenly Father, they could not survive emotionally. "The steadfast of mind You will keep in perfect peace, because he trusts in You."[1]

The believer's eyes were fixed on Him, and they had a glow about them. The nonbelievers were always angry, yelling and cursing in the streets, and they always wore a frown. When you look into many of their eyes, you think you are looking at the devil himself. Many worship the voodoo priest and truly are serving a false god. They are angry and lost with no direction in life. They steal, and it appears they do whatever it takes to get whatever possible for their own self-gratification. If I could have only shouted David's words from Psalms to them and made them to listen. "Depart from evil and do good; seek peace and pursue it."[2] Oh, if they just had ears to hear how much more peaceful life would be if they pursued Christ instead of their own desires.

While waiting at the bus stop, my husband saw a poor, elderly woman sitting peacefully, not bothering a soul on the back of an open bus. She had apparently made a trip into town to pick up a few supplies she needed and was on her journey home. A young guy came to her and tried to steal something from her, and she pushed him away. He then retaliated by coming and taking the gallon of kerosene out of her hand and threw it on the ground, busting it open. The women jumped off the truck and ran to where the kerosene was leaking out on the ground. She hurriedly stood the container up and found a piece of plastic nearby. She tried to scoop up the puddle of kerosene off the ground. Scoop after scoop, maybe a tablespoon at a time, until she thought she retrieved all she possibly could get back into her container. Mixed with dirt, she managed to scoop up about one-half of what she originally purchased. This small jug of kerosene was so precious to her. It may have been all she could afford for months.

My husband could tell she really needed and treasured the kerosene. His heart ached for this poor woman as he witnessed this encounter. Is this the kind of trial James was talking about when he said we should count all trials joy? I do not believe for one minute and neither did my husband that this woman was feeling overjoyed at this moment in her life. Was it a testing of her faith that would produce endurance? She sure was enduring a lot at the moment, and because of the violence in the area, not one man on her bus tried to help her. My husband wished he had been able to jump off his bus and run over and help this elderly woman scoop up her precious kerosene. I can assure you, this woman did not think what she endured had its perfect result since she would go home with one-half of her purchase and now it had a special additive called dirt. If my husband could have just run up and asked her if she felt perfect and complete, lacking in nothing, she would have said she was lacking one-half of her kerosene and probably smacked him in the head for not helping her. She felt empty-handed and defenseless. Her heart ached to the inner core. My husband told me this woman stayed calm through the entire incident. She simply went peacefully at the task of retrieving what she could of her kerosene and found peace in knowing she did all she could possibly do. The Lord gave strength to this woman, and the Lord blessed her with peace just like He promises He will do.

"The Lord gives strength to His people; the Lord blesses His people with Peace."[3]

Whenever I was around the Christians in Haiti, it was a completely different feeling. The peace that only God can give was a light to the world. I am sure they are concerned about their lives and their country, but they were more concerned about getting the Word of God out to those who did not have peace. They had a desire to keep the story of Jesus moving. They knew Jesus Christ had come to give them peace and to give it abundantly. There was enough to go around. Jesus was their peace, and they knew they had access to live peacefully in the Father's house. "For He Himself is our peace"[4]

The Christians I met in Haiti showed me the true meaning of this statement. He was their Prince of Peace, He was their All in All, He was their bright morning star, He was their beginning every day, and He was what they clung to as they lay down to sleep at night. "In peace I will both lie down and sleep, For You alone, O Lord, make me dwell in safety."[5] While in Haiti, I too had to lie down in peace and sleep, knowing I was dwelling in safety. I was protected by God. We slept with the door to the bedroom open to the outside every night. There was no security in the home at all, and at any time anyone could come and steal whatever they desired or harm us as we slept. The Lord had to give us peace to lie down and know we were safe with His protection all around us.

The Lord called my husband and I to make this trip and minister to the Haitians. I had to remind myself the Lord of Peace Himself will give me peace at all times and in every way. The Lord would be with me wherever I go and in whatever circumstance I find myself. This was a minor mission compared to what Moses had to do when God called on Him.

Imagine how Moses must have felt when the angel of the Lord appeared to him in the flames of a burning bush. Here he watched a bush on fire and yet it was not burning up. What a puzzled feeling he must have had, possibly even a little fear. Yet his curiosity got the best of him so he walks over to check it out. Once the Lord sees

Moses checking out this bush, God calls out to him from within the flames. A sense of peace must have comforted Moses for he simply responded, "Here I am." He did not turn and run from the Lord. I can only imagine if this happened to you or me. I think I would turn around and start running as fast as I could in the opposite direction if I saw a bush on fire and not burning up. If I later realized it was God, I may turn around once I calmed down and recaptured my senses, but my initial response would probably be to run.

Then God told Moses not to come any closer and to take off his sandals because he was standing on holy ground. He probably was not sure he wanted to get closer once he heard a voice from within the bush. After all, whoever heard of a talking bush bursting in flames? I can just picture him pulling off those sandals as quickly as he could and standing there barefoot while thinking, *What am I doing listening to this talking bush?* Regardless, Moses stood there in reverence to God. How often do you sit and squirm in your seat in church—your mind running off in another direction. You are thinking of what you will do after church, where you will have lunch, and just when this service will be over so you can get on with your day. Many Christians simply have not mastered a Godly reverence to the Lord nor gained the ability to peacefully stand before the Lord in His presence.

Look how Moses struggled after God identified whom He was, saying; "I am the God of your father, the God of Abraham, the God of Isaac and the God of Jacob."[6] A Godly fear came over him and he hid his face—afraid to even look at God. I think when many people get to heaven, stand before the throne of God, and have the opportunity to look into His face, they will want to hide their faces as well.

Oh, what a mighty God we serve! God looked down on the Israelites with compassion, and He saw the misery His people were going through. He heard their cries, and He was concerned about the suffering they were enduring. He instructed Moses to go to Pharaoh and bring the Israelites out of Egypt. God wanted something better for His people, and He wants something better for everyone today. God also wants something better for the Haitians living in misery and suffering. Oh, how I wished I had seen more peace in the streets of Haiti instead of chaos.

Moses had the same type of question we often have when God calls us to do mission work. "Who am I that I should go?" God's reply: "I will be with you." Moses had many other questions to which God always had the answer. He even gave Moses many signs and wonders hoping to relieve his disbelief and give him the peace he needed knowing that God would be with him. This would be no little task for Moses.

I remember when I was first asked to go to Haiti. I had a lot of the same questions and fears Moses experienced. I too wondered who was I that I should go and was I knowledgeable enough and equipped to go. I even pondered some of the same comments that Moses voiced to God, "Please, Lord, I have never been eloquent, neither recently nor in time past, nor since You have spoken to Your servant; for I am slow of speech and slow of tongue."[7] I wondered what I would say. How could I teach and lead? How could I work with an interpreter? I could not speak professionally enough. I would not have the right words. There were many other negative thoughts while I tried to talk myself out of going.

As I prayed about the mission trip, God gave me a peaceful feeling about going. In modern-day terms, I received the same response Moses received from the Lord.

> The Lord said to him, "Who has made man's mouth? Or who makes him mute or deaf, or seeing or blind? Is it not I, the Lord? Now then go, and I, even I, will be with your mouth, and teach you what you are to say."[8]

All I had to do was pursue peace and I would find it. I would have to treat it like a treasure and hang on to it throughout the trip and just trust God for the right words at the right time. I had no more excuses about the Lord sending another messenger; it was time I get out of my comfort zone and go.

When Moses finally started out of Egypt with the Israelites, the journey was far from easy. His road was also rugged, rough, and rocky like the one we traveled to get to Belami. They traveled by foot with the Lord ahead of them in a pillar of cloud as their guide and at night in a pillar of fire to give them light. Moses endured numerous times when the Israelites grumbled and complained. He simply took the issues to God. He would cry out to God, and he always received an answer. I have no doubt that as we went across mountain after mountain, the Lord was ahead of us clearing our path and guiding our way. Although I had heard of times when a group came to this same area and their lives were in danger, I started crying out to the Lord before I even left home. I felt peace as we made the journey.

We followed the river for miles and had to cross the river several times. I always wondered how our driver knew it would not be too deep for the vehicle and what if we fell in a deep hole and water got into the engine. Nothing compared to crossing the Red Sea on dry land with a wall of water at your right and your left. What if the wall of water broke lose? Moses knew God was with them, and I am sure he felt the peace of God with him as he led the Israelites across the Red Sea. He looked back as the walls of water broke, flowed back as normal, and swept away all of Pharaoh's chariots and army. Not one of them survived. I cannot even imagine the peaceful feeling that must have swept over Moses as he witnessed this great miracle from God and knew *His* provision remained with the Israelites.

The Israelites were so amazed by the great power the Lord displayed. They feared the Lord and put their trust in Moses, His servant. The peace the Lord offered was so prevalent that the Israelites, along with Moses, started singing a song to the Lord. Yes, you guessed it—as we continued our journey bouncing along the road, my dear friend on the mission trip with me joined in, and we too sang songs of praise to the Lord.

What happens next is even more puzzling to the Israelites. They were hungry and saying they should have just stayed back in Egypt in slavery because they at least had food to eat. How many times have you said; "Oh, if I only could have died rather than face this problem I am facing?" My friend, this is when God wants to step in and supply your manna from heaven. This is when God wants to give you enough food for today, tomorrow, the next day, and the next day—on and on forever. He will supply "all your needs according to His riches in Glory." It makes me just want to shout and let the whole world know God is available for anyone who will come to Him and take up residency in His house. *Praise the Lord!* No one is rejected if you just come!

I started writing this chapter and was right to the part I mentioned in the previous paragraph. Exhausted from a long day, I finally retired for the evening around 11:00 p.m. and fell fast asleep. At 4:00 a.m., I woke up with one of the most beautiful visual pictures in front of me I had ever seen. I was crawling across the floor. I started out on my hands and knees and then I was crawling on my stomach. Before me was a set of feet from the knees down and the tail end of a robe. I was trying so hard to reach the feet and touch the robe, but they were always one step ahead of me no matter how fast I pursued them. Then I knew, just like Moses knew, why he took off his sandals. He was in the presence of the Lord God Almighty. I continued to crawl after Jesus, and the words going through my head that morning were, *If I could just touch the hem of His garment.* I had no particular reason for wanting to touch except for the longing to feel His presence. I spent the entire day peacefully empowered by the presence of the Holy Spirit. Don't you think this is how Moses must have felt throughout his journey toward the land the Israelites were to inherit?

Although our journey was nowhere as intense (only one day rather than forty years) nor nearly as far as the Israelites had to travel, no suffering along the way, I knew the Lord was with us, and we would make it to our destination. After forty years in the wilderness with trials and frustrations, grumbling and complaining along with confused feelings, the people still pushed forward listening to what Moses had to say and pursued their inheritance. The Lord wants "to shine on those living in darkness and in the shadow of death, to guide their feet into the path of peace."[9]

You may be wandering in the wilderness right now, but know this, life comes after you have gone through the wilderness allowing yourself to transition and move on. While you are in the wilderness, you must allow yourself to be refined so you look to your Father and receive the peace the Father intended for you to have. The Lord wants to give strength to His people and bless His people with peace. You can move forward with confidence, living the abundant life in the Father's house. In Haiti, most of the Christians lived in the wilderness with little or nothing—totally dependent on God, and they were experiencing the glory of God that brings peace. God's manifest presence permeated their homes and churches.

Who was I that I can come to Haiti and what could I possibly do to make a difference in such a poverty-stricken country? Could I possibly have anything to say and share that would encourage and change any lives? A prayer for peace was where I started. Many people, including professing Christians, do not have the peace that surpasses all understanding embedded in their hearts. They have not chosen to completely depart from evil and do good and neither had many of the Haitians I saw.

Dear readers and friends, He himself is your peace (Ephesians 2:14) and if you have confessed your sins and accepted Jesus Christ as your Lord and Savior being justified through faith, you can have peace with God through our Lord Jesus Christ (Romans 5:1). There is peace living in the Father's house.

Study Questions

1. How do you think your life would be different if you walked day by day without any fear in your life?

2. Do you think it would make a difference if you went through life without complaining? Questioning God? Doubting what God is saying to you?

3. Have you made the decision to completely turn from evil and do good things only? Are you seeking peace and diligently pursuing it?

4. Just how do you go about pursuing peace?

5. Are you restless, feeling tossed around like the surf of the sea? Is your life kicking up the mire and mud? If so, come into the Father's house and find peace.

6. How often do you find yourself running away from God rather than running toward God?

7. Do you promote peace in your community or do you secretly stir up divisiveness?

6

Celebration in the Father's House

In Haiti, there were so many things to celebrate in the Father's house. The Haitians celebrate with excitement at seeing the walls being raised for the future church building that will protect them from the heat of the sun's rays beating down on them. They celebrate having guests to speak to them and enlighten them in the Word of God. They celebrate the gift of life God is providing for them, and they celebrate the fact they are able to obtain a printed copy of the Holy Bible. This happens because someone cares enough to send money to Haiti just for purchasing Bibles to distribute as gifts. A printed Bible is a treasured gift—not just a commodity to sit on the shelf.

In a country where people have so little, they still had many things to celebrate. To the Haitian Christians, nothing was more important than celebrating the greatness and glory of the Lord. They would come together and exalt His name together. Praise and worship time at every evening service was a big celebration. I sat in the service one evening thinking about church back home, perplexed by the difference in our excitement to celebrate. For many Christians in the United States, it takes special effort to celebrate the real reason for Christmas and Easter. We get caught up in decorating for these two holidays and getting trapped in the secular meanings. We forget the real meanings are the birth and resurrection of Jesus. Each individual has something worth celebrating every day of his life if he will live in the Father's house.

When we celebrate and magnify the Lord by reaching out to Him, we are able to gain a greater perspective of how big God is. The closer we allow ourselves to get to God, the more we are able to recognize just how He works on our behalf. There is always something to celebrate when Christians rely on God to meet their every need. In the outer areas where we were ministering, there are no doctors to run to when you are sick. Believers cry out to God and call on Him to be the Great Physician and celebrate when He heals. I had the opportunity to witness the miraculous healing power of God on several different occasions and see the celebration that took place afterward.

We had been invited to visit in a home where two people were in great need of a miraculous healing. They were facing death. One elderly lady in her eighties was lying in bed for over a week with an extremely high fever prior to our arrival. She was barely able to eat and was delirious. No one expected her to live much longer. When I touched her arm, she was hotter from the fever than I had ever felt anyone before. Her family was just ready to let her lie there and die because they had no means of getting her to a doctor who was hours away. They had no money to pay the bill. They had prayed for her, but the fever remained. Her daughter-in-law said she was not a Christian, and to the best of her knowledge, her only worship was to a voodoo priest. There was concern for her physical health but an even greater concern for her spiritual health.

The visiting pastor took a few minutes to talk with her through an interpreter and asked her if she served the voodoo priest. She merely grunted and acknowledged she did not believe in God and did believe in voodoo. I wandered if this woman would believe in the Lord Jesus Christ if He touched her body and healed her? If the god she served and prayed to did not heal her but the God almighty did, would she really believe? Then the real test came when the pastor asked her if she was ready to die. Her eyes glared at him, and you could see fear written all over her face. I could tell she was afraid of dying. He told the woman about Jesus and how He wanted her to confess that she was a sinner and served the devil. He said Jesus wanted her to give her heart over to Him, and He was the only one who could heal her. The visiting pastor also asked her if the voodoo priest was so powerful, why had his prayers not been answered and healing come to her body? After straining a few grunts from her frail voice, the pastor then asked her if we prayed with her and God removed the fever, would she believe in Him. She immediately responded with a quick yes.

Here laid this woman on her deathbed, barely able to feed herself, and yet she wanted proof there was a Savior. I wasn't sure she really meant it when she said yes, but I sure was hoping God would show up, touch her body in a miraculous way, and restore her body temperature to normal so her eyes would be open to the Almighty God who was able to save her soul. Although I had never met her until that day, my heart grieved for her lost soul and her disbelief in Jesus Christ.

Putting our faith into action, three of us laid hands on this woman as the pastor prayed, lifting her and the fever to the Lord. We wanted her physically healed so she would give her heart to Jesus and find spiritual healing. Her body temperature gradually became cooler and cooler. At first I was not sure if I was getting used to the heat her body was putting off or if my hand really did feel cooler skin under it. By the time the pastor finished praying, the fever was gone and her body temperature returned to normal. What a time of celebration as she started yelling out loud. She just kept shouting "Thank you Jesus, Thank you Jesus" over and over again. She raised her arms toward heaven and, with tears streaming down her cheeks, shouted, "Halleluiah, halleluiah, halleluiah." Tears streamed down my cheeks along with her as I celebrated the moment she gave her life to Christ Jesus. She could now live in the Father's house.

Like this woman who was astonished and amazed at what God had done, there were times in the Bible when the same amazement brought people to belief in Christ Jesus. One night when Paul and Silas were in prison and were singing praises to God, an earthquake shook the prison. All the prisoners could have run away because the chains fell off them and the gates rattled open. When the prison guard woke up, he was ready to kill himself, thinking he slept instead of guarding the prisoners and now he was in great trouble. Paul spoke up and told him not to harm himself because the prisoners were all accounted for, sitting right there in their cells. While they could have run, they stayed put. The guard then went running over to Paul and Silas, trembling, and fell down at their feet and asked, "What must I do to be saved."[1] The guard knew there was something different about the lives of Paul and Silas. Even while in prison, the two of them found reason to sing and celebrate the glorious Lord Jesus Christ.

Christ's works amazed people back then, and it has the same effect today. This woman was at the end of life and had nowhere to go except hell until the mighty power of God reached out and touched her. Until this day, she simply would not believe in Jesus but continued to put all her faith into serving a false god. Some people just will not accept the truth until it smacks them in the face.

My friend, Jesus, wants to touch people all over the world today. He wants to give you something to celebrate. He wants you to celebrate the all-saving power of the Lord Jesus Christ. He wants you to celebrate His birth, His death, and His resurrection and continue celebrating until His return to earth to gather up His children and take them home to eternity. We will celebrate forever when the bridegroom comes to get the bride, and we live forever with Him in paradise.

Another celebration occurred when we prayed over a Christian man suffering from a serious infection throughout his body. With no medicine, no antibiotics, and no gauze to cover the wounds, he laid on the concrete floor of his home on his stomach so the wounds on his back would not be irritated with merely a dirty sheet over him. It was just one year earlier he had given his heart to the Lord. Before, he worshipped the voodoo priest for years and was known in the area as a mean and violent man. On previous trips, the pastor said the mean and violent man would come to the evening services and disrupt the service and would attempt to cast spells on the missionary teams.

He suffered the loss of several of his children during the previous months, including a newly born baby. One day, while depressed and angry from these deaths, he began raging and crying out in anguish like he had done in the past. His friends thought he was turning back to worshipping the devil. They were sure he had gone crazy and lost his mind. They proceeded in attacking him and strapping him with ropes to a tree, fearing he was going to hurt someone. He was left there on the rocky ground strapped to the tree for several days until he calmed down. The church family explained to us he was not demon-possessed again but merely was screaming and crying out to God in all the pain he was experiencing from the loss of his children. He was hurt, angry, and grieving—asking God, "Why?" Listening to them tell how he was attacked and tied to a tree, left there for days crying out to God for mercy, I thought of how merciless the actions were to Jesus as well. This man suffered a minor portion of pain compared to being whipped, beaten, pierced with nails, and hung on a cross.

During the time he laid on the rocks, the sharp edges pierced holes into his skin. He was now seeping with infection from all those open wounds. The holes were so deep you could see the bone and muscle tissue. As they pulled back his dirty sheet, you knew without a miraculous healing or some medical treatment that this man was in trouble. The smell from infection permeated the air. Once we started to speak with him, he said he was ready to lie there until he died because he was going to heaven to be with the Lord. I think he almost longed to die just to be removed from his pain and be in the presence of the Lord. I can only imagine how Jesus must have felt when he hung on the cross fighting for His last breath—longing to go home and be with His Father in His house.

We prayed with this man, believing God had a plan for him and was not ready for him to die. We had faith God would heal him, and we expected a miracle. Once again, we put our faith into action with our works. James tells us in the Bible that faith without works is useless.[2] What good would our faith have been if we walked away and merely said, "We will be praying for you"?

As the pastor was praying for him, four more of us laid hands on him, and in agreement, we all lifted him up to the Lord for healing. Curiosity killed the cat, and it was killing me as we prayed for the gentleman. I had the faith, and I wanted to witness the healing touch of Jesus on this man's wounds. I kept my eyes open expecting to see this man healed as prayers were lifted up to God. What I witnessed before my eyes was amazing. I blinked a couple of times to be sure my eyes were not playing tricks on me. Once I even removed my glasses and wiped the lenses then put them back on to be sure they were not fogged over giving me blurry vision. I watched two of the holes start to close up and get a glaze over them. I could see skin closing in on the exposed muscle and bone. Two of the spots were now very shallow, small openings glazed over.

I wondered why there was not complete healing. Why not finish the job. Of course God has His own plan, and it was not my place to question what God was doing. The still-small voice in my head said this is just the beginning, and he will be healed. A plan was devised to carry this man out of the woods, down steep terrains, over rocky paths for hours to get to a location where they could put him in a vehicle and get him to a doctor for some antibiotics. I witnessed a prime example of the body of Christ in action. God could have healed the man completely, but the outcome would not have been the same as seeing the native men pull together in love scrapping up all their resources, carrying him over miles of land to show him how much they cared and reach out in love. The royal command mentioned in the book of James, "You shall love your neighbor as yourself,"[3] must have been the motto of this group of men. One simply stated, "We cannot leave him here like this, he needs medicine to totally heal these wounds, let's do whatever it takes to get him to a doctor." I think they loved their neighbor as much as they loved themselves and maybe even more.

All healings are not immediate, but we have to trust God that He will give us a second touch and continue to touch us until we are completely healed. Once when Jesus entered the city of Bethsaida, friends of a blind man rushed to bring him to Jesus. They knew Jesus could touch him and heal him. Jesus took the blind man outside the city gates where the two of them were alone together, and He touched the eyes of the blind man. He asked the blind man, "What do you see?" Jesus could have touched the blind man and brought him instant healing but chose not to. The blind man responded with an answer that lets you know full vision was not restored. Then Jesus touched the blind man's eyes once again. This time he clearly saw.[4]

Although I had celebrated in my own heart and prayerfully thanked God for what I witnessed, the group celebrated the next day around the dinner table. My husband popped the question, "Did anyone see what I saw yesterday while we were praying for the man with the open wounds?" It turned out I was not the only one with my eyes on the wounds. The pastor then laughed as he said, "So, I was not the only one watching?" We all laughed as we realized we had all been watching, believing in faith and expecting to see a miraculous healing. What I had written in my journal the previous day really did happen. I did not have blurring or cloudy vision. We all chuckled and praised God for the great things He had done.

Within two weeks of returning home, we received word the third spot that was very large in size was healing beautifully. This gentleman went on to full recovery and was back witnessing for the Lord. What would have happened if no one took the time to pray for this man? What if no one took the time to carry him out from where he lived to medical treatment? What if no one had shared his or her financial resources to help a poor child of God? My heart is grieved at the lack of generosity the majority of people in the United States have. We live in a world where it is all about *me*! What can I buy myself, store up for myself, and do for myself, leaving the poor to remain poor.

Although the Christian Haitians were poor in a worldly sense, they were rich in Christ and had something to celebrate every evening. At the beginning of every service, the people celebrated by praising the Lord through songs of praises; then they lifted praises to the

Lord in prayer. They praised God when a word was spoken they were in agreement with, and they praised Him at the end of the service when people came to the front of the church for prayer. Praise and honor to the Lord never stopped during the service, and I am sure, as many of the Haitians walked home from the service, they were still celebrating.

    We have freedom living in the Father's house. "It was for freedom that Christ set us free; therefore keep standing firm and do not be subject again to a yoke of slavery."[5] Jesus Christ came into this world so we could be set free, and you need to grab hold of this. Stand firm and claim it and never turn back. You can celebrate every day once you realize the Spirit of the Lord God is upon you. Isaiah prophesied, saying, "The Spirit of the Lord God is upon me, because the Lord has anointed me to bring good news to the afflicted; He has sent me to bind up the brokenhearted, to proclaim liberty to captives and freedom to prisoners."[6] Christ Jesus will set you free and you can celebrate that freedom—bring good news to others, bind up those who are brokenhearted, set the prisoners free. Celebration is an everyday event when you put your life into action for Him.

Study Questions

1. What does your faith look like to others?

2. Do you have works to go along with your faith? Can you celebrate the goodness of Christ Jesus by seeing your faith in action?

3. Do you take time to celebrate when you see God at work?

4. Do you celebrate even when things do not go your way?

7

Love in the Father's House

In the area of Haiti where we were ministering, most of the local people only had one meal per day and went without any food the rest of the day. They only had rice and black beans or whatever was ripe in their gardens at the current time. Some families had chickens for eggs and a pig for meat running around in their yards, but with the limited supply of water and feed, the animals were very thin. Whatever the Haitians had they were willing to share with us to be sure we were taken care of the best they could. The love they showed us overwhelmed me because it was more sincere than I generally experience with Christians at home.

One morning as the women came out to the morning session, one lady carried with her a tiny plastic basket lined with a piece of fabric. Inside this basket were two eggs she must have gathered before coming to the meeting at 6:00 a.m. You could see the love in her eyes as she handed the basket of eggs to one of the leaders. She gave from her heart, and she gave all she had. Reflect on the story in the Bible found in Luke 21 of the widow's offering. She too was very poor. She gave all she had to live on, and she gave from the heart. Jesus said her gift was greater than the wealth given by the rich. The rich could give easily because they had plenty left over, but the poor widow gave her best keeping nothing for herself. Her love was so great for Jesus that she put Jesus first, herself last, and others in between.[1]

Every time you passed one of the ladies in the street or after every session we taught them, they would all hug and kiss us on the cheek. They would line up and wait their turn to hug you and hang on to you like you were a precious jewel. I received more hugs in ten days in Haiti than I do in ten years from women in the church in the United States. The women of God had purified themselves and had fervent love. "Since you have in obedience to the truth purified your soul for a sincere love of the brethren, fervently love one another from the heart."[2] The love you felt was from the heart, nothing fake or put on for a show, but genuinely felt from their souls.

Genuinely loving from the soul is lacking among believers. We live in a society where jealousy, discontentment, pride, and many other things stand in the way from loving like we should. The Lord wants to make your love increase and overflow for each other until it just flows out like rivers of living water. John commands us to love each other as Christ has loved us[3], and this is a pretty high standard that requires continuous work. Our love is to be sincere, without hypocrisy, and devoted to one another. The only debt we are to owe one another is to love them, and the women paid their debt every day as they came and showed their love.

The Christian Haitians demonstrated God's love to those around them—not just with words but also with deeds. They recognize truth in scripture and put the principles in practice. "Whether, then, you eat or drink or whatever you do, do all to the glory of God."[4] Without having television, radio, video games, and other distracters, they immerse themselves in work, scripture, and prayer. The one thing that entertains them is church. It just adds to their knowledge and dependence on Christ Jesus. In the United States, we curl up on the couch reading a great novel, but in that area if they read any book, it is a Bible. I did not see any other books or magazines around. Haitian Christians seemed deeply rooted and anchored in Christ. They know He is their only source of survival. Jesus is all they have to depend on, but in the United States, we have too many things that keep us from having dependence on God. Most of us have more food than we need, shelter, clothes to wear, doctors available when needed, and many distracters.

To love the way God intends for us to love, we need to practice self-denial on a regular basis. For most of the Haitians, it is an everyday occurrence. For us, a good way to start is through fasting. Fasting is training your heart, soul, and mind to do without something. What you give up draws you closer to God and provides many rewards. Every home I visited while in Haiti had no television, no computers with online social networking, no telephones, barely any food—so they do not have to think really hard about what to give up. Think about all the items that distract and consume time that could be spent seeking an intimate relationship with the Heavenly Father. Practice giving up some of the time you spend wastefully, dedicate yourself to God instead, and watch your life change. As your love for God grows, then your love for others will grow.

While we hustle from work, friends, children's activities, school, and recreation, the people in Haiti are building relationships. They are connecting with one another's lives, taking time to care and share, affirming each other and keeping community life grounded. They have not bought into the philosophy that individualism provides a better, more-fulfilled life. They know being grounded cannot happen without a community of friends. All around them is a corrupt and broken world. They have to resist temptation and practice disciplines that keep them grounded in Jesus. They have to remain submerged in an active community of loving and faithful believers on a mission for God. They have to be available to pray with others when sick, to soothe brokenness in each other's personal lives to offer a glimpse of hope when others feel it is all gone, or to offer support in any needed way. This in return supports the unity of the body of Jesus Christ described in scripture. They become the hands and feet for Him, keeping the work of Christ going. They endure suffering together rather than laugh and let you thrive on your own.

I saw far more dedication in the Christian village in Haiti than I have ever seen or experienced at home in the United States. While I much rather enjoy the life I live in the United States without being so poor, I admired the oneness I felt while there. During one short week,

I felt like part of a community—part of their body incorporated into the body of Christ. Oh how we have gotten away from being unified and doing our part, serving and loving the body of Christ compared to areas like this one. Yet we say we live in the Father's house. Our focus and our lives need to change to live in the Father's house—to experience the direction and correction the Father wants to give us.

Americans are so independent and strive for individualism in our society while in Haiti it is the opposite. Instead they strive for a community lifestyle. Children are playing together in the streets with homemade toys, and women are helping each other cook and do chores in the sweltering heat. If someone has no place to sleep, another invites him or her in. They take in each other's children for the night if they have no home. When not working, you may see several people gathered up on a front porch sharing moments together. This friendly circle brings support and life to one another as they open up their hearts to one another. Now remember, this is what I saw in a community of common faith, otherwise they have to help each other look out for thieves.

They developed a healthy community of love by working together and serving one another in love. I could see them sharing and sacrificing what little they have and even being inconvenienced to help meet the needs of others. This is a picture—a true example of what life is like in the Father's house. They have developed the key ingredient to creating a community-based way of life. It is the way God would desire each person to act. When people learn to develop community—loving and serving each other, then and only then will they be connected and reach their full potential in the Father's house.

In the church I attend, we are all challenged to seek God and determine a ministry we are gifted in and called to do—jumping forward and putting our gift into action. Many have ministries in the workplace or some other area outside the walls of the church site. They have applied their gifts along with faith to broaden the community. The outcome is awesome when you look at each of the various ministries and how each one has extended the community in general. By reaching others, the love of God is shared with many. This is what life looks like in the Father's house. Our souls should long for more and our minds should open to new paths and new approaches to show the love of Christ to a lost and dying world.

"If, however, you are fulfilling the royal law according to the Scripture, 'You shall love your neighbor as yourself,' you are doing well."[5] Jesus's half brother James tells it like it is. We are programmed to be in love with ourselves, and we spend more of our time caring for our own needs. It would be wise to evaluate how much time you spend taking care of yourself, loving on yourself, and compare it to how you reach out and love your neighbor. I think most of us would be surprised. Read the words once again, it is not just a law, it is a "royal law." I took time to look up royal in the Encarta dictionary and the definition says it is "relating to, belonging to, or consisting of a king, queen, or other member of a monarch's family" or "of the most excellent kind." Well, this law no doubt relates to a king and belongs to a king—but not just any king. It belongs to the King of kings! And it is without a doubt of the most excellent kind. Other than loving the Lord your God with all your heart, soul, and mind, there is no greater command than to love your neighbor as yourself.

This command was important enough that it was mentioned several times in the New Testament. Here are a few other verses where you read this royal law.

> Owe nothing to anyone except to love one another; for he who loves his neighbor has fulfilled the law.[6]

> For you were called to freedom, brethren; only do not turn your freedom into an opportunity for the flesh, but through love serve one another. For the whole Law is fulfilled in one word, in the statement, "You shall love your neighbor as yourself."[7]

Look back at what James says at the end of the verse. If you love your neighbor as yourself, you are doing well. Out of submission to

God and your love for God, you should love others. Remember the old saying; "The love in your heart wasn't put there to stay, love isn't love till you give it away."

Study Questions

1. When you look at how you love others, are you doing well?

2. Some of you may say you do not love yourself very much. It is time to see yourself the way God sees you. We are commanded to love one another as He loves us, and the only way this can be accomplished is to see the real you through God's eyes. Can you fathom the love the Father has for you or do you struggle with acceptance?

3. Are there things that you need to reconcile with God? Love cannot be fully accomplished if you hold back reconciliation.

4. Do you find yourself judging others rather than loving them? Negative judgment will prevent you from loving others.

8

Intimacy in the Father's House

If we would all compare our intimate relationship with God to how we handle our relationships with our spouses, our children, the people we work with, or close friends, we would no doubt be surprised at how little time we spend building the intimacy with God. Every relationship takes work, time, understanding, trust, communication, and commitment. In my book *Lost in the Wilderness*, I shared how I had come to a time in my life where I could see all the great treasures I found in my earthly father. I never truly accepted these same treasures from the Heavenly Father. These treasures were easy with someone I could feel, see, and spend time with every day. The truth is, I realized it is the same with God. I can feel Him, see Him, and should spend time with Him every day. It was up to me to accept His love and build the relationship. He was available if I would just spend time in His presence getting to know Him.

"I will be a father to you, and you will be my sons and daughters, says the Lord Almighty."[1] He is one Father that you do not have to question whether He wants the intimate relationship with you. The choice is yours. He says He is our father and we are His children, and it doesn't get more intimate than that. The question is, are you accepting the relationship or running away from it? Intimacy with God has no competitors. God Himself wants to give you abundant life, and once you embrace this truth, you can build a more intimate relationship with Him.

> God sent His son, born of a woman, born under the law that we might receive the full rights of sons. Because you are sons, God sent the Spirit of his Son into our hearts, the Spirit who calls out, "Abba, Father." So you are no longer a slave, but a son, and since you are a son, God has made you also an heir.[2]

If we have full rights as a child of God and we are one of his heirs, we have the ability to have an intimate relationship with Him. In this verse, it does not sound like God our Father is keeping anything He has from us so if you are a member of the family, an intimate relationship is available. You simply have to be willing to build the relationship just like you would with someone you were dating. When you date someone, you want to spend as much time with the person as you possibly can. You can hang on the phone and talk for hours, share your secrets with them, you give them gifts, you would go out of your way to please them, you show the person respect, and many other things to show them you love them. Somehow intimacy with the Father often does not get the same treatment. Very little time gets spent with Him. Prayers, which are our phone conversation, are short, our gifts are few, we don't go out of our way to please Him, and we trample all over Him time and time again rather than show respect.

Intimacy in the Father's house can be so much more if you want it. Intimacy in the Father's house creates a special bond that you are able to share with Him. It is so personal that many times you simply cannot explain the things you encounter. You feel them in your heart but cannot describe them to others. Accept your relationship with God is personal. Be patient and let it grow, knowing it takes time just as it does in our relationships with others.

It was time and hot pursuit to know God that allowed a man by the name of A. W. Tozer to develop an intimate relationship with the Father, experience living in the Father's house on earth, and spend eternity with Him. He became a Christian at the age of seventeen. He had an insatiable hunger and thirst for the things of God. Soon after becoming a Christian, he cleaned out room in the basement where he spent many hours praying and meditating on the word of

God. His only tools for learning were hours of prayer before God and notebooks from early Christians and theologians. He became a well-known Christian author of forty books and pastor of several churches, staying at the first church for thirty years. Having never attended college or seminary, Tozer received two doctorates. All of this was accomplished by his desire to seek an intimate relationship with the Father. He allowed the Holy Spirit to teach him. He quickly learned that nothing gives you more freedom than intimacy with God. I believe God has so much more to offer to all of us if we just pursue our intimate relationship with Him.

To build intimacy with God, we have to first be honest with God. We cannot lie to God. If He knows everything, why do you think you can fool God and be dishonest? We have to build a trusting relationship with God. You have to trust Him at His word. You have to trust His promises are true. You have to trust He knows what is best for you and be willing to obey Him. You simply have to be vulnerable to the relationship and open up your heart. We have to learn to understand God. In order to accomplish an understanding of who God is, you have to spend time in His Word, reading about Him and spend time communicating with Him. Even Jesus had to spend time alone with God. "But Jesus Himself would often slip away to the wilderness and pray."[3] Jesus needed time alone with the God and would go to quiet places to be alone with his Father. We need to do the same thing. We must spend time in prayer, being honest with God, and building a relationship with Him. When spending time talking and praying to God, just tell Him what is on your heart and in your mind. Without praying and talking to God, it is not possible to have an intimate relationship with Him.

There were many children of God in the church in Belami that obviously had an intimate relationship with the Father. People can tell when someone spends extended time seeking God. You can feel the presence of God when you are around them, and their faces are radiant with the glory of God. Our last service was on a Sunday morning before leaving Belami for the journey back to Port-au-Prince.

Excitement filled the hearts of Haitians as they came together one more time to praise and worship the Lord. The leaders planned on ending the service by having communion. It was different than what I was used to at home in my church. The Haitians did not have the nice-polished silver racks with individual cups for each person filled with grape juice. Instead, beside the unleavened bread were two pewter cups full of wine. Faces of the people were glowing as they looked forward to an intimate time with the Heavenly Father.

The message was winding up, and the time arrived for the communion service to begin. There was a much more serious feeling in the Father's house. It was not a time this group took lightly. Individuals were asked to examine themselves and confess anything hindering their relationships with God. By the serious looks on their faces and the reverence in the place, you knew they were truly looking and questioning their lives, making sure there was nothing hindering the intimate relationship between the Father and themselves. Some had accepted Jesus but had sin or even a question of sin in their life so they simply passed the plate on to the one beside them and did not take a piece of the bread. When the cup of wine was handed to them, they motioned with their hand once again and did not participate in the intimate celebration with God. They knew that if their relationship was not in oneness with God, then they would be mocking the seriousness of the elements of communion. The bread and the wine as elements resembling the body and blood of Jesus meant something to them.

They passed the cup from one to the other, took a sip, and passed the cup on to the next. They had no concern about passing germs in an area of the world where many deadly viruses could be spread. If one person's lips or fifty rested on the rim of the cup, it was perfectly okay. No time for worrying about germs—this was an opportunity to share in the precious blood of the Lamb, to feel intimate and one with Him. I knew in my heart, as many drank from the cup, it had a powerful meaning to them. You could see it in the expressions on their faces. It was a blessing to share in the blood of Christ. The cup did resemble the blood of the new covenant poured out for mankind.

It was a serious moment, a celebration, a time of thanksgiving, and a moment of sheer intimacy with the Father for sending His one and only precious Son as a sacrifice for us. After the cup went across the lips of several hundred people, it was a pleasure to put your own lips on the rim of the cup and sense the intimate moment with God. Not only did He send His Son to live on earth, facing every temptation we face, suffer far more than we ever will, He also allowed Him to shed His blood, be beaten, mocked, pierced with nails in His hands and feet, and hang on a cross He had to carry for His own death so that we might be saved. Knowing all this, it would be merely mockery to take communion without an intimate, personal relationship with Him.

Many churches celebrate communion and do not take its meaning as seriously as they should. Small children who do not even understand what it is about participate and others living in sin also participate so they do not stand out in the crowd. It did not seem to embarrass one person to pass the bread and cup as compared to the consequence of putting up a front and pretending they were close to God when they were so far away. In most cultures, too much pride stands in the way of an honest heart. People would rather mock God and put on a front, hoping no one knows the truth, rather than be honest with themselves and the world. I even thought of all the years I was not rightfully in the position to commune with God, to acknowledge our intimate relationship because I was weak and had a shallow friendship with minimal loyalty and devotion.

When I lost my father, I spent a long time feeling completely displaced and simply feeling lost. Without my father, I struggled day after day knowing I could no longer pick up the phone and call him. I could no longer share conversations with him, no longer cry on his shoulder and the many other things a healthy father-daughter relationship offers. During this time, I would spend hours talking to God, listening to God, and reading the Bible. I was learning more of

His attributes, His personality, and learning to better communicate with Him. I realized every time I talked to God, I was just like the "daddy's little girl" I was to my father. He always seemed to know what I was thinking, when I was hurting, how I was struggling, if I needed an answer, and, of course, He always knew when I just needed an ear to listen. I was working on the intimate relationship with my Heavenly Father. I was learning "with all prayer and petition to pray at all times in the Spirit."[4]

You can feel the Lord if you simply want to. If you draw near to God, He promises He will draw near to you.[5] This means God wants to get cheek to cheek, eye to eye, up close, and personally intimate with you so you can feel His presence. He wants you to feel His touch when you are in need, to know His arms embrace you when you need someone to hold you up, and He is always available no matter what day or hour your need arises. If He is such a great friend, how could anyone take the elements resembling the sacrifice of Jesus Christ, the covenant made to His people, so lightly? How could we have lost the meaning of communion?

Here in Haiti, the meaning was not lost. Those who did not have an intimate relationship with the Father through His Son, Jesus Christ, did not participate (I cannot guarantee all, but the feeling was in the atmosphere). The pastor shared with us why they passed the communion elements on and the seriousness they took in the event. It was as if they feared the Father and did not want to mock Him. Jesus says in John 6, "I am the bread," and they could not take the bread if they were not one with Him. It was a reverent time before the Lord for those who knew Him. They did not worry about each having their own sanitary little cup. They took a sip from one of the large cups, and it was passed on to the next person. They were willing to share in drinking the blood of the Lamb and be unified one with the other as well as being one with Jesus Christ. You could glance at their faces, and you knew they had intimacy with the Father.

An intimate relationship is available to everyone if they want it. Intimacy is a privilege freely given to everyone by Christ in His sacrifice on the cross. "God is faithful, through whom you were called into fellowship with His Son, Jesus Christ our Lord."[6] Since Jesus is God in the flesh, the intimacy you develop with God is with Christ Jesus as well. When you commune, you are accepting the ultimate vulnerability of God in Christ who humbled Himself by death on the cross. When we humble ourselves with God, true intimacy will begin. Are you willing to humble yourself and seek true intimacy with the Father and start living in His house?

Study Questions

1. Do you have an intimate relationship with the Heavenly Father?

2. Can you think of ways to improve your relationship with Him?

3. Do you spend enough time talking to God and building your relationship? Do you take time to listen?

4. Do you humble yourself before Him on a regular basis, allowing your relationship to increase?

9

Joy in the Father's House

"The thief comes only to steal and kill and destroy; I came that they may have life, and have it abundantly."[1] You can also experience a life filled with joy living in the Father's house. Jesus came so that we can have an abundant life full of joy. Your mind cannot comprehend the abundance of joy God has for you. We live in a fast-paced world experiencing many hardships and trials along the way. The enemy is continuously lurking around looking for a way to steal, kill, and destroy the joy in your life. I have experienced times in my own life when I allowed Satan to steal my joy before I had even realized it, and I am sure you have as well. While doing ministry in Haiti, I witnessed Christians living an abundant life full of joy and happiness regardless of their circumstance. With very little as the world would measure wealth, they were richly blessed with joy. I came home with the realization my joy was shallow compared to what I witnessed. I learned that I needed to press deeper and deeper into the river of joy that Jesus has for me.

Haitian Christians found joy in the pure and simple delight of just being alive. They were deeply satisfied by simply knowing they were able to serve others. They quickly responded to feelings of happiness and experiences that brought them pleasure and were aware of the abundant life they had in Christ Jesus. It seemed to come completely natural to them because of their faith, gratitude, love, and hope in Christ Jesus. I felt as if they simply invited joy into their lives, and there it was. Simple little things made them happy; they would go throughout their day enjoying life rather than enduring it.

I had a hard time imagining how they could be so happy with the hardships they faced every day. They experienced sadness and sorrows on a regular basis, and even when the tears are flowing down their cheeks, I believe they accept them as stepping stones leading them to a greater joy.

I will never forget the smiles I saw on their faces as the local people came out of the woods watching and looking around. They were excited that visiting missionaries were in the area. There was joy on the faces of children running up to see the missionaries as they picked up our pace and walked along the road beside us, chattering with each other all the way. Word spread the week before. With great joy and anticipation, people eagerly awaited, and now the time had come. The children knew why we had come, and they were delighted.

Why are we not eagerly waiting upon the Lord the same way? Why do we not anticipate His coming? Why are we not running up and down the streets announcing the coming of the Lord? My friends, we are missing the true joy we should have in the Lord. Your joy in the Lord is your strength,[2] and we should be delighted in the Lord.[3] You can find joy in seeking Christ Jesus for He is your source of Joy.

I specifically remember the delight and joy I saw in the children. They would stand by the fence at the edge of the yard where we stayed and just watch and stare for hours. We would show them attention, and their faces would light up with joy. Joy came from the simplest things as children ran barefoot up and down the rocky roads. They would chase the one motorized vehicle they have probably seen in months as they giggled and squealed. They just wanted to see it, to hear the engine, to touch it, and hopefully catch a glimpse inside. They hoped in their hearts to be able to beg a ride even if only for twenty feet down the road. They wanted the joy of saying they got to ride in a vehicle. We see vehicles as a common commodity, and unless we are excited about getting a new automobile, it is not something that we laugh and squeal over. We quickly discount the daily joy that we get out of having this luxury to take us where we need to go. We simply take it for granted. The joy of the children made me wish I had a jeep or some type of vehicle to ride the children up and down the road all day.

The only toy I saw in my ten-day stay was the rim of a plastic container rolling in circles led by a stick with a piece of a metal coat hanger on the end. The children would walk pushing on the stick to make the rim roll in front of them. This homemade toy was only available to children lucky enough to have a metal coat hanger and a lid from a five-gallon bucket. I threw away many wire coat hangers from the dry cleaners, but there it was part of a precious toy. This was a great toy, and it brought joy to the children walking behind it. I was reminded of the excitement and joy most American children have opening presents on their birthday or Christmas morning opening gift after gift with great excitement. Within a few days, the newness wears off, and they wonder what they can have next. Their joy wears off quickly because they have so much. One of the ladies on the team shared an experience of handing out lollipops to the children, and after they unwrapped it, they did not know what to do with it. She had to unwrap one herself and show them it was something to eat. She was amazed at the faces of these young children as they enjoyed the flavor of the lollipops dissolving in their mouth.

On the day of our departure from Belami, I passed off most of my clothing to the women and left with an empty suitcase. The women liked to wear skirts since they were cooler, and they especially like to wear skirts to church. Many of the women did not even own a skirt, so it was a joy to have one simply given to them. They were so appreciative. I must have heard a thank-you more than a dozen times. Their willingness to share with each other and not add to their own wardrobe amazed me. Each woman would only take one outfit so another woman could have one as well. There was no need for closets in their homes, because if you were lucky, you might have a change of clothes while one is being washed and dried. With the abundant amount of clothing I had back home, what I left would never be missed. It was a treasure to the Haitian women and a joy to be able to share.

After being in the company of some of the devoted Christian Haitians, I truly believe they take refuge in God. I believe they say to the Lord, "I am no good apart from you." I believe they felt empty without God, and nothing else could bring them satisfaction like Jesus. I was amazed as I observed how they entrusted their lives wholly on God while living in such poverty. Many people would think God simply let them down when they are without food, shelter, and little or no clothing to wear. We need to remember, "The kingdom of God is not eating and drinking, but righteousness and peace and joy in the Holy Spirit."[4] It was obvious they recognized their life was hopeless without God, and they were desperate for Him and found great joy in His presence.

Christ Jesus is worthy of our pursuit because He is the source of all joy, and it showed in the life of the Christians I was around in Haiti. It brought to mind Philippians 3:7–9,

> But whatever things were gain to me, those things I have counted as loss for the sake of Christ. More than that, I count all things to be loss in view of the surpassing value of knowing Christ Jesus my Lord, for whom I have suffered the loss of all things, and count them but rubbish so that I may gain Christ, and may be found in Him, not having a righteousness of my own derived from the Law, but that which is through faith in Christ, the righteousness which comes from God on the basis of faith.[5]

Yes, they may want more things than they have, but they would much rather have Jesus. They think Americans have too many things distracting them from their relationships with Christ Jesus. Instead of hours in front of the television or on the computer, they are reading the Bible or praying. It was easy for me to see why they smiled and were filled with the joy only Jesus can give.

Jesus lived a fun-filled life as well as a life of preaching and teaching. Many times He attended parties enjoying the company of others.

He was even accused of being a drunkard and a glutton from time to time simply from having a good time at a party. The Bible tells us that before the cross, Jesus was anointed with the oil of joy above His companions.[6] Jesus no doubt was a very happy man, and we can have this same happiness when we come into the Father's house and pursue His Son. The Christian life does not mean you live in misery and unhappiness, never having any fun. God wants people to be full of joy and enjoy life.

Many people look at joy as a mere happy feeling, but as Christians, it is much more. In the world, lost people think Christians are miserable people who never have any fun. I see it just the opposite way and think the sinfulness in lost people's lives make them miserable people. They may be having fun at the moment on the surface but are definitely missing a heart full of joy.

> If you keep my commandments, you will abide in My love; just as I have kept My Father's commandments and abide in His love. These things I have spoken to you so that my joy may be in you, and that your joy may be made full.[7]

Jesus wants His joy in you. He desires the obedience that just naturally comes out of an intimate relationship with Him. Do not let your joy be threatened by disobedience to God's word. This is Satan's way of stealing your joy. When you desire Jesus alone, seeking Him above everything else, you will find true joy. Nurture your joy so you do not lose it from the pitfalls of life.

Joy is one of the blessings you receive living in the Father's house. I love the way John Piper explained joy in one of his messages.

> Joy in Christ is the good feelings in loving Him and believing in Him. It's the echo in our emotions—our hearts—of experiencing Christ as precious and experiencing Christ as reliable. It is the deep good feelings of being attracted to Him for who He is and the deep good feelings of being confident in Him for what He will do.[8]

As Christians we need to love Christ, believe Christ, and rejoice in Christ with joy inexpressible and full glory although we do not see Him.[9]

Take every possible measure to protect yourself from being deceived by all the false ideas floating around about how to find true happiness and joy as a Christian. Start with the list of nine ways in Matthew 5, which include being pure in heart, being humble, being gentle, being a peacemaker, hungering for righteousness, and having an eternal perspective about life. Christ instructs us to have joy at all times even when persecuted for His sake. Circumstances may make it hard to find happiness and joy at times, but if you let the kingdom of Christ rule in your heart, invest in the heavenly priorities putting your faith in Christ rather than the earthly circumstances, you can find fullness of joy.

As Christians, happiness should stem from our hope in the Lord even when the tears are falling, when we are suffering, when we are in pain, or when we experience trials of any kind. A believer's joy is not some fake politeness, a fake smile, or a fake act of caring. Joy is a condition of the heart, and it gives you strength to carry on being faithful regardless of your circumstances just like I witnessed in the Haitian Christians. They had joy living in the Father's house and knew God's joy will endure forever. Be confident in your Heavenly Father and decide to have His joy. Choose to be mistreated along with the people of God rather than to enjoy the fleeting pleasures of sin.[10] Any joy derived from sinful pleasures is merely temporary. God promises joy to His children so the battle is whether you believe God's Word or not. Sometimes you will be filled with joy even without asking, and at other times in your life, you may need to fight for it. But always know it is available.

Study Questions

1. Why are Christians not eagerly waiting for the Lord to show up in their lives?

2. Why do you think many Christians are not anticipating His coming?

3. Do you find joy in seeking Christ Jesus? How do you obtain the joy Christ made available to you?

4. What does a life of joy look like to you?

5. What are the characteristics of joy? What makes joy beautiful? What makes joy ugly?

6. Do you recognize the importance of avoiding dirty, unclean and ugly things? Can you think of things of this nature that bring or brought you joy?

7. Is your joy being covered by worldly distractions? If so, is it because you have taken your eyes off of Christ Jesus and your personal relationship with Him?

10

Instructions in the Father's House

We are told "All scripture is inspired by God and profitable for teaching, for reproof, for correction, for training in righteousness; so that the man of God may be adequate, equipped for every good work."[1] From the beginning of time, God's people followed His instructions or suffered the consequences. It begins in Genesis 3 when God made Adam and Eve. God gave instructions not to eat from the tree of the knowledge of good and evil in the middle of the garden, telling them if they did, they would die. Satan, in his craftiness, convinced Eve she would not die but would instead have her eyes opened and be like God, knowing good and evil. I am sure the fruit was brilliant with color and just the sight of it made her mouth water. It no doubt looked delicious and tempting. Then to think she could gain wisdom by eating it. Wow, what could make it more tempting! Giving into the lies, eating the fruit, their eyes were opened, and they at once realized they were naked. They covered themselves the best they could and tried to hide from God because they knew they had done something wrong. People still think they can do wrong and hide it from God and avoid the consequences. It is simply another way Satan tries to deceive people into believing God does not mean what He says, but the Bible clearly says that God does not change.[2] So if He said it—it is true!

In the second book of the Bible, Exodus 20, God spoke and delivered ten laws or commands to Moses. The first one instructed people to have no other Gods before Him. God is it! The second is to not make for yourself any idol. Idols can be anything you worship, love, fear, or serve above God. This command is meant to reveal God's leadership and limitless love. The third is to refrain from misusing the name of the Lord our God. While you may not curse God, dishonoring Him in any way is also misuse. The fourth command is to remember the Sabbath and keep it holy. Even God took time to rest after creating the world in six days. He sat back on the seventh day to rest, and He wants us to do the same. Without proper rest, you can have biological, physical, and emotional effects. The fifth command is to honor your father and mother. It is the first commandment with a promise attached. God tells us to honor so you live long in the land He is giving you. Then we are instructed not to murder but to preserve life instead, not to commit adultery which includes any sexual sin outside of marriage, not to steal, not to bear false testimony against your neighbor, and not to covet anything belonging to your neighbor. You need to be happy with what God provides for you and not want what someone else has. These are the same commandments Jesus later proclaimed to everyone in the New Testament, and He advanced the rules even further.

The Bible was given as an instruction manual to show mankind the love of God and show you how to live your life. It is God revealing His truth to all mankind, and He wants to make sure you know the way to live pleasing to Him. God would not expect you to enter into a new way of living as His child without instructions to guide you. If you are going to live in a different culture, as a Christian, you need guidance, and this is why we have the inspired Word of God.

I watched as the Haitian Christians poured into the church site, willing to sit in the heat uncomfortably for many hours seeking instruction. They were willing to soak up as much teaching as we were willing to give. It did not insult them when you corrected them because they wanted to learn the right way and were willing to make changes. They longed to be adequately equipped for every good work God instructed them to do. Their hearts and minds continued to be renewed and cleansed as they listened night after night. I looked out over the crowd and watched the tears trickle down the faces of those once again broken before God. This brokenness was conditioning their hearts. The heart is the main organ in the circulatory system. To live, your heart has to function properly and propel blood throughout the entire body. If your heart fails to work, you simply cannot live. To live like Jesus, your heart has to be conditioned and routinely cleansed then the love of Jesus will be propelled to the world around you. If your heart is not properly conditioned and functioning correctly, you will not be adequately performing the work God has for you.

Having experienced a change of heart, it put them in a spiritual position to be the salt and light in their village. They were radiant children of light beaming for others to see Jesus in them. I could pick the Christians out in a crowd because they stood out from their peers. Salt seasons, purifies and preserves, and their testimony was like salt seasoning their community in Godly ways. They were always prepared to share Christ to everyone by words and actions. They fought against evil, preserving what belongs to God, which was no easy task in an area full of evil practices and teachings.

Eager to learn, the women came early every morning for instruction. After our time of teaching and sharing, we opened it up for questions at the end of each session. The women would ask question after question because they really wanted to understand. They were struggling to live life from one day to the next and had a lot of questions for God. They had many broken relationships among their neighbors, many of the women were bitter from sexual abuse or rape, many did not feel loved, some struggled with how to love others, and much more. They struggled to understand life itself. Trying to understand how and where God was in the midst of it all was overwhelming. The women longed for instruction and guidance on how to overcome their situations and love unconditionally.

Since I was one of the leaders, I was up front and facing the crowd. I was able to see the serious looks on some of their faces. Nothing seemed to distract them from intently listening to whoever was sharing instructions for living in the Father's house. When it was time for the service to be over, they mingled together like they never wanted it to end. Many still did not have a copy of the Holy Bible, so getting instruction from a preacher, teacher, or relying on the Holy Spirit to teach them was their way of learning. Hundreds of Bibles were purchased for the area, trying to place one in the hands of anyone who could and was willing to read it. If all the answers to your questions in life are found in this one book, it is important for everyone to have a copy. Jesus became flesh and showed us how to live and left this perfect instruction manual to use for reference.

The Bible reveals many ways to live out life successfully. As you read and study the Bible, He gives instructions on how to live your life pleasing Him. Without instructions, you could not even understand why you need Jesus. There are detailed instructions for followers of Jesus Christ to direct every area of your life. Many instructions are found in six chapters in the book of Matthew.[3] In these chapters, you can read instructions for all areas of human conduct, including your attitude, your business practices, financial pursuits, things acceptable in husband-wife relationships, children-parent relationships, and friend-enemy relationships. You find instructions on having proper motives rather than strictly doing things out of obedience and detailed instructions on how to follow the nature and character of Jesus Christ in the world in which you live. God also instructs you through others He sends to bring messages (through teachers, preachers, and prophets). God may visit you in dreams or in visions or simply place thoughts into your mind giving you direction. He has the instructions for every question you could possibly ask, and you merely have to seek for the answer.

In Haiti as well as everywhere else in the world, Christians living a defeated life simply do not understand the instructions that Jesus left for them. You may be one that understands and knows the instructions but chooses to be disobedient without even realizing you are a citizen of the kingdom of Heaven. Some people struggle trying to fit into the world and be accepted by being like those in the world rather than living in obedience. As Christians, you live in the kingdom with Jesus Christ. He is the King of the kingdom and His instructions are important.

If you are a Christian feeling defeated, start with following the greatest commandment in the Bible, "Love the Lord your God with all your heart, and with all your soul, and with all your mind."[4] When you truly love the Lord your God, you will want to please Him by following His instructions. You will want to know and understand as much as you can and look like one of His children. Next, move on to the second greatest command and "Love your neighbor as yourself."[5] You can be so in love with yourself and trying to do everything to please yourself that you forget your neighbor even exists. When you show others love, they are able to see Christ in you. It is easy to follow the instructions laid out for our lives when we have the level of love these two commands are calling for. I sensed the Haitian Christians had the right attitude. They had renewed hearts desiring to keep all of God's commands because of their love for God and obedience to these two greatest commandments. They had a deep desire to see things go well with them and their children forever.[6]

It is impossible to reap the full benefits of the kingdom if you do not obey the instructions pertaining to kingdom living. Haitian Christians hunger for instructions to teach them how to live successfully with God, their family, their environment, and their community. I did not see a lot of pride or selfishness standing in the way of their willingness to be obedient. They know they will not experience full joy that God provides for success on earth without knowing the rules and following them. He promises joy to your house if you hold fast and stand firm to His ways.

While Haitian Christians looked for instructions on how to live by kingdom principles, many Christians do not. For some Christians, it is easier not to look because then you have an excuse for not obeying. Jesus Himself said, "man shall not live on bread alone, but on every word that proceeds out of the mouth of God."[7] If the Christians living in the area we were ministering in counted on bread alone, I am sure they would become quite discouraged. I even watched one mother mixing dirt with food for her children just to help fill their stomachs. Some days they had nothing to eat at all, so trusting God to provide their needs like He promised out of His own mouth was their only means of survival. God's promise of provision was a way of life to them.

Jesus knew we need instructions and guidelines to live by. It all starts with repentance and having faith in the Lord Jesus Christ then understanding the benefits of living by the instructions. We are promised wisdom to understand the Word of God and knowledge of how to apply the principles to our own life. Jesus came so we can have abundant life, and this is accomplished by functioning here on earth as we follow Jesus's instructions for living. We live in a safe haven on earth if we follow His instructions. I felt the Haitian Christians knew they lived in a safe haven on earth. There would be no earthly way to feel safe and secure in their environment without Jesus Christ. Meekly they submitted to their difficulties, knowing God is in control and working all things to good.

The Bible says; "If you belonged to the world, it would love you as its own. As it is, you do not belong to the world, but I have chosen you out of the world. That is why the world hates you."[8] I observed that as some accepted Christ as their Savior, they were completely ready to put off the old, ready to move out of the old lifestyle in the world which was falling apart, leaving behind all the dirt and filth. They were ready to move into the Father's house, living in an environment with a full set of instructions. Their desire was for their acts, deeds, and behaviors to look like citizens living in the Father's house. Once you reside in the Father's house, you no longer belong to the world, and you need to avoid pleasing the world or striving to fit in by compromising the Father's instructions in any way. He has chosen you, taken you out of the world, and placed you in His house.

Jesus said, "Truly, truly I say to you, unless one is born again he cannot see the kingdom of God."[9] Jesus was not referring to natural birth but goes on to explain, "I tell you the truth, no one can enter the kingdom of God unless they are born of water and the

Spirit. Flesh gives birth to flesh, but the Spirit gives birth to spirit."[10] You can understand instructions in the Bible pertaining to life in the kingdom if you are part of the kingdom. The Holy Spirit is our helper whom the Father sent to teach us all things, and the Spirit will teach us truth. Jesus Himself knew the importance of the Holy Spirit because He said it was better for Him to go so the Helper, the Holy Spirit, could come.

Instructions teach us to be men and women of integrity without hidden motives, striving to bring resolution to conflicts regardless of who is guilty and allowing the Holy Spirit to flow through you bearing fruit. Following His instructions requires you to stand firm for Christ even when persecuted. The Christian community needs rules and regulations to accomplish God's intent. Without specific instructions, our lives would be chaotic, and we would not function properly. God knew being born again into the Body of Christ would require instructions about how to live and grow in your new spiritual position. For this reason, He sent Jesus who gave all instructions needed to live and grow in your Christian life. Life becomes beautiful when you belong to God and follow His instructions. Everything in the kingdom is accomplished by following instructions. If someone had not been obedient to God, there would be no preachers, evangelists, teachers, or anyone else doing work to build the kingdom of God. I would not be writing this book if not for obedience to God as I do not even take time to write letters. Writing is not something I personally set out to do, but when God says, "write," and the words pour out on the pages, in obedience I simply do it.

When you are in a position to pass on instructions from the Word of God to someone else, be sure to understand the truth yourself. Study and observe the words of God together. Do all instructing in love without condemning the person in any way. Always lead by example and gently guide the person allowing God to work in their hearts. After you point out God's instructions, be sure the person knows how to apply what he learns to his life. Instruction without understanding produces no gain in knowledge.

Study Questions

1. Do you have a deep desire to know the Father's instructions?

2. Are you living in compliance with the instructions given by Jesus, or do you pick and choose the rules commands suitable to you? If not, what excuses do you make for not following God's instructions completely?

3. What holds you back from digging deep to find all the instructions for living in the Father's house where you reside?

4. In Matthew 5:3–10, you find detailed instructions on what will bring you blessings. Do you understand what it means to be poor in Spirit, to mourn, to be meek, to hunger and thirst for righteousness, to be merciful, to be pure in heart, to be a peacemaker, and to be persecuted for Christ? Study these verses and define the meaning of each one. What benefits do you receive by following His instructions?

5. How can you demonstrate you love God? How do you show other people you care about them and love them?

11

Praise and Worship in the Father's House

"Come, let us go up to the mountain of the LORD, to the house of the God of Jacob. That He may teach us concerning His ways and that we may walk in His paths."[1] Every evening around five, we started walking up the dirt trail to the mountain church site to praise and worship the Lord and teach His ways to the Haitians. Praising and worshiping the Heavenly Father had no time limit in the church in Haiti. Unlike people in the United States, there were no thoughts about getting out the door for lunch. They don't sit in their seats pondering to which restaurant they are heading for lunch nor do they think of all the other things they want to accomplish after church.

The service would start with praising and worshiping God for approximately two hours followed by preaching for at least one hour. After ministering to all who responded to the invitation, the service would come to a close singing and praising again. After every song and prayer, they would all shout, "Thank you, Jesus." They could not thank Jesus enough for the splendor and majesty He holds. Sometimes they would say, "Thank you, Jesus," over and over again for three to five minutes with hands lifted toward heaven. They were truly thankful from the bottom of their hearts, thankful for who God is and for all He has done. They directed their praise toward God and were thankful for the splendid brightness of His presence.

I do not want to leave you with the impression everyone in attendance was praising God in this manner, but the Haitians, who had an intimate relationship with the Father, understood the definition of praise. Some of the American Webster Dictionary definitions include: "to express approval of, to express admiration of, to applaud, to magnify in song or to glorify." There was no doubt their expressions of praise proved they admired and approved of who God is. Their voices magnified God in song, and they applauded God many times. Their praise was vocalized and well heard as their voices echoed throughout the area.

Some in the congregation kept their mouths shut, afraid to lift their voices to God, while others had no relationship with God at all. The prophet Isaiah said, "To get yourself up on a high mountain and lift up your voice mightily—to lift it up and do not be afraid." You should not worry what your voice sounds like, if you carry a proper tune or if you know all the proper words. God is not looking for perfection; He is simply looking for praise even when you do not feel like praising. The greatness of God never changes. You have to be determined to praise Him regardless of your feeling or circumstance.

The Haitians would praise God, singing song after song with hands raised high or waving in the air. They wanted God to hear their voices as they cried out to Him with hands lifted high.[2] They lifted their hands to the sanctuary and blessed the name of the Lord.[3] The lifting up of hands was their evening sacrifice.[4] Feet were tapping to the rhythm of the music, bodies swayed from side to side, and some danced with one another before the Lord. Everyone moved about as they praised and worshipped God.

"I stretch out my hands to You; my soul longs for You, as a parched land."[5] On this mountain and in love with the Lord, it was impossible for my soul not to long for the Lord, to yearn for His presence and thirst for Him. One evening, I had a beautiful vision as I listened to the voices of the group singing. It was a quick glimpse of what it must be like in heaven. I could see various tongues, tribes, and nations bowing at the feet of Jesus and praising and worshiping Him. The voices were absolutely beautiful as they echoed out in various languages but all singing the same tune. Tears flowed down my face as I continued to praise and worship God with my Haitian brothers and sisters. Some tunes I recognized and sang in English as they sang in Creole. During some songs, the power of the Holy Spirit took over my voice, and I could sing right along in Creole and know the words they were singing. I had asked the Lord to please allow me to praise and worship with them and know what they were singing before going to Haiti. He provided this opportunity. Why not ask, knowing it will be given? Why not seek and know you will find? We do not have because we do not ask in faith, believing it will be given to us. I asked, believed, and I received. Praise the Lord!

The last evening as we came together in the house of the Lord to rejoice and praise God, a three-year-old girl captured my heart. What I witnessed was true praise, truly from the heart, nothing made up, and nothing put on for a show. It was a lovely toddler lifting up holy hands before the Lord. She did not care who was watching, she did not notice anyone around her, and she was genuine before the Lord. If you would simply become like a little child before the Lord, what a difference it would make in your praise. God has commanded you to praise because it places you in a proper relationship with Him and brings changes to your life.

Like every other evening, many children sat in the front of the church, singing and praising God, but this little girl was different. She glowed from head to toe. When they started singing the first song, a three-year-old girl sang right with them. She did not miss one word as they sang for over ninety minutes. You could see the feeling in her expressions as she sang her heart out to the Lord. I could hear her voice over the other children. I could feel power released from her singing as she clapped her hands, sang to God with cries of joy, and sang praises to our King. A true example of a few verses found in Psalm 47, which read,

> Oh clap your hands, all peoples; Shout to God with the voice of joy. Sing praises to God, sing praises; Sing praises to our King, sing praises. For God is the King of all the earth; Sing praises with a skillful Psalm.[6]

Her feet never stopped moving as she danced before the Lord in perfect rhythm. She sang with her hands raised toward heaven as if she was reaching out to touch Him. She was drawing close to God and coming into His presence. Sometimes she would have one hand on her heart and one hand raised toward heaven with her head looking up and eyes closed as she worshipped and praised the Lord. She already had a heart for Jesus and would praise him with more enthusiasm and spirit than many adults. She was not ashamed to sing, dance, shout out to God, acknowledge, and praise Him, and she did not care if it was perfected or who watched.

Later, the local pastor asked the congregation to pray for the missionaries to have a safe trip home and to thank God for bringing them to Haiti. As each one spoke his/her own prayer aloud, this little girl did not miss out on this opportunity either. She glanced my way and noticed my gaze on her as we exchanged smiles. Then her eyes were shut, head tilted toward heaven, hands raised high. This toddler started praying out loud and did not stop until the entire crowd had stopped. She was already emotionally and intimately involved as well as physically involved in her worship and praise time with the Lord. With her head raised to God, I am sure this young child was releasing joy to the Father of her house. Certain her simple words carried a powerful meaning—I wished I could have understood what she was saying as she prayed to the Lord. At the end of her prayer, I could hear her shouting, "Thank you Jesus, thank you, Jesus, halleluiah and amen." (A few of the words I learned to recognize in Creole.) She was learning to talk to her Father at a very young age.

By this time, I just wanted to hold this precious child in my arms. I really would have liked to pack her up and bring her home with me so she could show children and adults in our church how to praise and worship God. I could not resist any longer, so I held out my arms for her, and she ran into them. I hugged and hung onto her for several minutes before I could let go. As the music started once again, we just danced together and praised the Lord hand in hand.

When the message started, she curled up on my lap, exhausted from two hours of dancing, and fell fast asleep. She was as lovely as an angel with a brilliant glow. I felt like I held a jewel in my arms, a jewel I never wanted to lose or let go of. Her skin was soft, and she had a skinny frail body. As I held her in my arms, I started to cry while praying over her. I claimed her life as another Esther, an Esther for today and an Esther who would come to the aid of her people. God has a specific plan for this child, and she has a destiny with Him. God is preparing another lovely young lady with a heart after Him. I prayed the Lord would use her to help share Jesus Christ and lead many people to the saving grace of God as she grew up and that the Lord would use this child to touch the lives of many in the mountainous region in which she lived. I asked God to start teaching her, molding her every day, and filling her with all the wisdom and knowledge her mind could conceive. I asked Him to let her continue to show others how to praise and worship God in this heartfelt manner.

This young toddler already knew how to praise God. The Bible has a lot to say about using our physical bodies in praise and worship. It is a sacrifice pleasing to God. The Bible tells us to sing, speak, shout, raise hands, and dance before the Lord. In the book of Psalms alone, there is more than fifty times we are instructed to speak and shout yet many Christians keep their mouths shut—afraid someone will think they are foolish. My friends, the only thing foolish is holding back your praises to the Glorious God and Father if you live in His house.

When it was time for a leader to pray, it was not enough for the Christian Haitians to just listen. Each one started praying to God privately, drawing closer to the heart of God. They were worshiping God through communion and fellowship. While everyone was incomplete and unworthy, they still came into His presence, seeking the face of the Most Holy God. They each wanted to show their gratitude to the Lord. No one was afraid to worship God in his or her own way. There was no embarrassment, no shame, or any distraction that bothered them. They were in the Father's house, and they could worship Him any way they wanted. They had gathered together as one body releasing His power through worship.

Worship was meaningful and heartfelt. Worshiping God had no time limit and could not be contained in a box. It was free because the Spirit of the Lord was in the house. Some stood while others fell to their knees before the Lord. The gates to the Godhead were opened through praise, and the Holy Spirit began to stir in the hearts of men and women. Worshiping God was allowed to take place as long as the Holy Spirit was moving among the people. No one had anywhere to go as soon as it was over except home, so why not linger in the Father's house. It was more comfortable being with fellow worshipers in the Father's house. In the Father's house, they could lay down their burdens and find prayer support. They could shut out the world and all its problems and just come before the Lord, worshiping and praising Him. Most evening services would last from 5:00 p.m. to 9:00 p.m. or later.

Whether you realize it or not, all human beings are made to worship. We chose whom and what we will worship, but we will all worship something or someone. Many people do not even recognize what it is they do worship because they do not understand the meaning of worship.

> But an hour is coming, and now is, when the true worshipers will worship the Father in spirit and truth; for such people the Father seeks to be His worshipers. God is Spirit, and those who worship Him must worship in spirit and truth.[7]

This is a very clear instruction given by Jesus directly. You may be wondering how worshipping in spirit and truth looks. Worshipping in spirit is allowing the Holy Spirit to energize your worship—to bring life to your worship. It is letting go of self and becoming alive with the Spirit. The Holy Spirit brings vibrant changes to your daily praise and worship time if you simply allow Him to do it. After all, if you are born again and are filled with the Holy Spirit, let His presence glow through you.

Worship God for who He really is. Don't try to make God what you want Him to be. Let Him be the one and only true God you worship and praise. Allow your praise and worship time to be a time of growing in your relationship with Him. Come before His throne with the idea that you are spending this time with Him and Him alone, and bring Him your most dynamic reverent worship. Learn to worship God in the hardest of times as well as the good times. The Haitian Christians live among many negative circumstances. For many, their lives are complete emotional turmoil yet they still acknowledge the supreme Lord. Rather than sitting back feeling sorry for their lives and the situations they are in and telling God how much He doesn't love them, they sit in the service, blessing and praising the name of the Lord and tell Him just how good He is.

It would be more than wonderful and ever so pleasing to God if, while you are in the tough situations and trials of your life, you could simply go to the throne of grace and worship the Lord. That type of expression from the inner depths of your soul shows God just how much you trust in Him to move you through the trials with victory. Remember what James said: "Blessed is the man who perseveres under trial; for once he has been approved he will receive the crown of life which the Lord promised to those who love Him."[8] My friend, hang in through tough times—get through the trials—worship and praise God no matter what and receive the crown of life. Don't complain and delay your worship to God during the difficult times in your life.

The Bible has stories of people who worshipped regardless of the situation they were in. Consider how Abraham must have felt when God commanded him to take his son Isaac up to the mountain and offer him as a sacrifice. Here he was making plans to kill his only son and heir whom God had miraculously provided. He gets all the necessary items together and takes two young servants with them as he starts out on the journey. Along the way, Abraham surely had disturbing thoughts and questions running through his mind. He probably questioned God's intentions and felt like God was deserting him. When they arrive at the foot of the mountain, Abraham tells the servants to stay with the donkey while he went with Isaac to worship God. Obedience and worship to God was Abraham's top priority. Could you be obedient to God if you were in this situation?

David (another example), known as a man after God's heart, had been fasting and praying for the life of his son for seven days. He spent his nights lying on the ground because his son (born out of his affair with Bathsheba) was cursed of God and lay dying. On the seventh day, the child died, and his response was anything but what you would expect. Although devastated from the loss of his son, David gets up from the ground, goes and takes a bath, puts on lotion and a clean change of clothing, and goes into the house of the Lord to worship. He did not jump up and down shouting, praising, and dancing before the Lord with excitement during this period of grief, but David did acknowledge the Lordship of his God. He knew God was in control, and whatever God chose to do was right.

Consider how God's servant, Job, responded after he received more bad news in one day than imaginable. In one day, he had his camels and oxen stolen. All his sheep were killed. His camels were carried off. His servants were murdered. And then, if that was not enough bad news for one day, he gets another message informing him his sons and daughters were killed when wind came across the wilderness and struck the four corners of the house and it fell on them. This no doubt was the worst day of Job's life. Rather than cursing God, Job gets up, tore his robe and shaved his head, and he fell to the ground and worshipped. You may wonder how anyone could worship God with all this bad news. I have to wonder myself. Job did not blame God for all the disasters even when his friends tried to convince him it was the sin in his own life that brought on all his trouble. Instead, he worshipped the sovereign God he served. When disasters strike in your own home, do you blame God or can you still praise and worship Him knowing He is in control of your life?

When Moses took the stone tablets to Mount Sinai a second time and presented himself to God on the top of the mountain, the Lord descended in the cloud and stood there with Moses telling him how compassionate and gracious He was, how slow He was to anger, and how abounding He was in loving kindness and truth. Moses was so overtaken by the presence and words of God that he bowed low to the ground and worshipped God. Joshua was by Jericho when he lifted up his eyes and looked. A man was standing across from him with his sword drawn in his hand. Joshua went to him to ask if he was for them or against them. The man said he had come as captain of the host of the Lord. Joshua fell on his face to the earth—bowing down before the Lord. These are just a few of the many examples throughout the Bible where people bowed down and worshipped the sovereign God we serve. Acknowledging the supreme Lordship of God Almighty should take place regardless of the circumstance you find yourself in. He is God in the good times, and He is God in the bad times. Bless His name at all times. If worship is an expression of love for God, it should be our soul's passion by nature. True authentic worship incorporates our thoughts and feelings together, causing us to focus on God in pure adoration. It is the same principle applied in Matthew 22:37, where we are commanded to love the Lord our God with all our heart and with all our soul and with our entire mind. The Father is seeking for us to be true worshippers and worship Him in spirit and truth.[9] You can't worship without the renewing of our minds. We are instructed "to offer our bodies as living sacrifices, holy, and pleasing to God-for this is your spiritual act of worship."[10] Through your worship, you express your love for God and your soul's passion.

Study Questions

1. Be honest with yourself and list who or what you are worshiping? Remember it may be more than one thing or person.

2. How do you become like the God you worship? If your heart is where your treasure is, where is your time and effort spent?

3. Is your praise and worship time monotonous or is it vibrant and filled with intimacy with the Lord?

4. Do you find it hard to worship God when you are going through trials in your life?

5. During the difficult times in your life, do you cry out to God for help without taking time to praise Him?

6. When disasters strike in your own home, do you blame God or can you still praise and worship Him knowing He is in control of your life?

7. With the numerous times the Bible instructs us to sing, shout, raise hands, and dance before the Lord, why do you think most people still sit or stand still while singing in a group setting? Are you embarrassed to freely express your feelings to the Lord?

12

Comfort in the Father's House

While making preparations for this mission trip, Satan began to attack some of the team members who were planning to go to Haiti. Anytime someone is moving forward in service for the Lord, the devil begins to attack. Wouldn't it be great if we simply had to plan to do great things for God and could sneak it right past Satan? Imagine what it would be like if we could see God work wonders and just laugh when Satan showed up too late? I am not sure about you, but it seems every time I am getting ready to do some form of ministry God has given to me, I go under attack. This is what my husband and I experienced along with another couple preparing to leave with us. Many obstacles were put in our paths—problems with work, issues within the extended families, and a multiple of other distractions. We had to take comfort in knowing we were in the will of the Lord and in Him we would find the strength to plunge forward.

One couple joining us in Haiti felt God was calling them to go into mission work full time. They were both very excited about making this trip and being servants for the Lord. The second day this man was going to preach the message in the evening service, Satan started to really attack. He had been given a message on the hatred of Satan, and I can assure you that Satan did not want it preached. Satan did not want to hear someone throw him under the rug.

As we arrived for the evening revival service and started singing praises to the Lord, his wife started feeling ill. She felt weak and sick on the stomach. Sitting in her chair, you could see the color in her face quickly fading. I spoke with her and asked if she needed to step outside and get some fresh air for a minute, and she acknowledged that she did. As we approached the doorway leading out the side of the church, I started to feel her body dropping. Knowing she was going to faint, I merely laid myself down slowly on the ground and let her fall gracefully on top of me to cushion the fall. The ground was hard and rocky, and I knew I could not let her hit it hard. Within seconds, one of the Haitian women bent down and picked her up in her arms and carried her out the door into the night breeze.

Her husband quickly came and was right behind us, wondering what had caused his wife to faint. She had never fainted in her life prior to this time and was in good health. Realizing Satan was trying his best to keep the message from being preached, I encouraged him to go back inside and preach the message the Lord had given him to share. We would take care of his wife and avoid allowing Satan to win at his games. Reluctantly, he returned to his seat, and the entire congregation stopped to pray for his wife while others helped get his wife down the mountain and into her bed to rest. Every time she woke up, she fainted again. This happened for three or four times before she was able to stay alert and focus.

Back on the mountain, the church was praying, and the comfort the prayer brought to this young man was the type of comfort only the Father gives. These men and women of God were lifting her up to the Lord and trusting God to protect her and heal her. At the bottom of the mountain, his wife was placed on her bed, and the local bishop and about eight women of God started singing a praise song to God. They were sending the music forth first to prepare the way for the prayers to follow. The women laid hands on her and prayed over her. Although I did not know what they were saying as I said my own prayer, I could feel the power and presence of the Holy Spirit all around. Then the Bishop took out a bottle of oil and had everyone anoint her with oil and pray once again.

As she started to wake up, I took her by the hand and just held her. I could see the comfort in her eyes. She knew the Lord was with her as she heard these women continue to pray for her as they walked around the outside of the open room where she lay, still praising and praying to God. I too felt so much comfort even though we were in a completely strange environment with no doctors within hours of driving. It was a comfort you could not possibly have if you did not live in the Father's house. You have to know the Father and live with the Father to feel the extent of the comfort He was pouring out.

Shortly, we could hear the echoes from the top of the mountain as her husband brought forth the message and rebuked Satan for over forty-five minutes. He was comforted knowing Satan did not win. Even with the distraction and not knowing how his wife was doing down the mountain, he had full comfort and peace only the Father can give. In the Father's house, He alone is our rock and our salvation. He is our fortress, our divine protector, and you can take refuge in the Father if you live in the Father's house.

Minds and hearts are clear of unbelief in the Father's house. If you doubt God can provide, you are living in disbelief. The Father is faithful and does not change because of our lack of faith. The Father's desire is to permeate our lives with blessings, and our disbelief can stand in His way, keeping us from receiving all He wants to bless us with. If we are convinced God will not deliver, provide, or heal, we will not see the miracles He wants to provide for us.

We are instructed in the Bible to cast all our cares upon the Lord because He cares for us, and I do believe He means all. Comfort is available beyond what we can possibly imagine, but we have to go to the Father when in need and allow Him to comfort us. Think for a moment of the words in Psalms 23.

> The Lord is my shepherd, I shall not want. He makes me lie down in green pastures; He leads me beside quiet waters. He restores my soul; He guides me in the paths of righteousness for His name's sake. Even though I walk through the valley of the shadow of death; I fear no evil for you are with me; Your rod and Your staff, they comfort me. You prepare a table before me in the presence of my enemies; You have anointed my head with oil; my cup overflows. Surely goodness and loving kind-

ness will follow me all the days of my life, and I will dwell in the house of the Lord forever.[1]

As you pluck this passage apart and you look at what it means for the Lord to be your shepherd, you will see it is a greater honor than you imagine. The duties of a shepherd are very burdensome and heavy. Shepherds are required to get up very early in the morning and lead forth the flock from the fold, or he would delegate the work to his children or relatives. The shepherd will try to avoid having a hired hand attend the flocks because they tend to neglect or abuse them while family has a personal interest in the well-being of the animals. God also has a personal interest in our well-being and wants to lead us forth.

David starts out with "The Lord" knowing He is the one and only shepherd who can bring comfort and peace. Lord is a term for master and owner, and you need to recognize God as master and owner over your life. He needs to be elevated to the highest position in your life at all times. The Lord "is" is referring to the present time. Like David, you need to remember God is your comfort and provider, and He is personally with you. When we experience the good times in our life, we often tend to forget to hold His hand while other times we are holding on as tightly as we can possibly grasp. "My" is acceptance of the fact He is yours personally. If you have an intimate relationship with the Father and live in His house, you have rights to claim Him as yours. Your relationship with Him might have its ups and downs like any other relationship, but know it is yours.

At the first sound of the shepherd's call (usually a peculiar sound hard to imitate), the flock would follow the shepherd to new feeding grounds. In the event two shepherds would call their flocks at the same time and the sheep had intermingled, they never mistake their master's voice. Let God be your "Shepherd." Listen to what God has to say about you and do not follow men's plans for your life. God is a loving shepherd who wants to lead you in the right direction. David selected "The Lord is my shepherd" most likely so He could remind himself of God's goodness and comfort. Is He your shepherd?

"I shall not want" does not mean God will give us everything our ego wants, but I do believe He is letting us know He will supply all our needs if He is our shepherd just like a shepherd tends to his sheep. The shepherd would march ahead of the sheep to a spot where they were to be pastured for the day. The chief shepherd made sure they were at a spot where they would have plenty to eat and at least once a day (generally around noon) lead them to a place to drink. The shepherd had to lead them to running streams of water or wells dug in the wilderness furnished with troughs. After drinking, the animals would lie down or huddle together in a shady spot of a rock, and the shepherd would take this opportunity to sleep. David acknowledged "He leadeth me." It is important to allow God to be your shepherd and lead you throughout life. He will lead you through the ups and downs in life. He will guide you in the direction of righteousness, giving you paths that are wholesome and filled with integrity. He will restore you when you fail or are reminded of past failures.

Psalms 23 goes on to say David had nothing to fear because he knew God was with him. He knew God would provide. When you walk through difficulties in life, you have nothing to fear. The Lord is with you. Just like a shepherd carried a rod and a staff to guide the sheep and to ward off predators that would harm them, the Lord has a rod and His staff. When you are prodded at times, it may be for your own good to keep you on your path. It may be for the protection of others, or it may be for protection from your enemies. Most of all, remember "the rod and staff" are there to comfort you and let you know you are cared for.

In biblical days, anointing the head with oil was a practice used to honor a person and show dignity to a person. "Thou annointest my head with oil" means you will be honored, dignified, and deeply respected as a child of the Father. "My cup overflows" is assurance God will give you even more than you need or can possibly use. You will be abundantly cared for and loved beyond your needs or wants, and you will have plenty to share.

"Surely goodness and mercy will follow me all the days of my life" lets you know wherever you go and whatever you do, goodness and mercy will go with you. At times you will sin, but if the Lord is your Shepherd, you have this statement of future protection, and you will be treated mercifully.

"I will dwell in the house of the Lord forever." It is your choice to dwell in the house of the Lord. You have to make a conscious decision to dwell in His house. You can focus your attention on the Lord, live by His set of rules, submit to God's will, and live with Him forever. While this may not be a physical house, it is a place to abide, embrace, and be one with the Father.

While in Haiti, I could simply sense comfort around the Christian Haitians. With the level of poverty and lack of resources, the Haitian Christian's level of dependency on God was the only place they could find comfort. They could not find comfort in food, houses, clothing, nor any other material possession—simply comfort in the loving arms of the Heavenly Father. They apparently made the conscious decision His house is where they will dwell. We all need to find comfort from God. At various times in our lives, we need and experience trials in which we feel the comfort God gives greater than other times. When I lost my father, God comforted me. I could feel and sense His presence as I went through the months following his death.

Now ten years later, the need for an abundant outpouring of God's comfort came to me in a new way. Yes, His comfort was there for me many times throughout the past ten years, but I had to pursue comfort much harder this time. The crisis left me feeling abandoned by God's comfort. I knew God's promises were true, and I knew God would see me through it because He still had work for me to do. Yet I could not seem to fight the loneliness and painful grief I was experiencing. I knew I had to cry out and depend on God and find hope and comfort from God's Word. I needed to recognize and deal with my anger and frustration. I was willing to trust God with my circumstances, but I struggled with seeing anything from God's perspective.

In My Father's House

It all began in November 2012, when what seemed like a brief trip to the pediatrician's office with my thirteen-year-old granddaughter turned out quite differently. What her mother thought to be a urinary tract infection ended up undiagnosed at the doctor's office and an immediate trip to Brenner's Children's Hospital in Winston Salem, North Carolina, one hour from home for a blood transfusion. One week into the hospital stay, I watched my granddaughter become weaker and sicker, getting more blood, and still no diagnosis. All we knew at this time was that her kidneys had been damaged and were failing with a high keratin level. Specialists ordered a kidney biopsy to send off for diagnosis to see what was going on in her body.

The second week, preliminary test results came back, and we were informed she had lupus or a form of autoimmune disorder in the lupus family. Treatment for lupus would begin the next day to try and put it into remission. The final report came back six days later, and the final diagnosis revealed severe kidney damage along with possible damage to other organs in her body. She had a rare autoimmune disorder called Wegener's granulomatosis. She would immediately need to start six monthly treatments of chemotherapy and begin taking a super high dosage of steroids in hopes of putting the disease into remission. After her first treatment, three and one-half weeks after admission, my lovely granddaughter was released to go home. Weak and with a very weak immune system, she was forced to be a homebound student. I watched her smile become a frown, her joy turn into sadness, her athletic body become frail, and her hope for a bright future dim along with much more.

I cried out for comfort and for knowledge on how to comfort my granddaughter. She was such a social person and found her joy in making others smile and from being involved in school. She longed to be with her friends, to laugh and smile and simply be around her treasured friends. Very few friends even came to visit since they were busily involved in activities with others, and her world became empty. Her friends from church did not see the need to spend time with her as their world went on and hers seemed to be caving in. I prayed and prayed along with many of my Christian friends and searched for comfort in the Word while spending time comforting and consoling her.

Several months passed, and I remember her asking me why none of her friends even came to visit her. She was learning a hard lesson in life; one I hoped would make her see the value of being a true friend to others rather than just seeing them as an acquaintance. It is easy to overlook our responsibility to comfort others in the same manner Jesus brought comfort to so many people along His journey. We tend to think what we have to offer is unnecessary rather than realizing that many times throughout our lives, God will use us to bring comfort to others. While He is our *comfort* and *strength*, we are called to comfort and strengthen others in our daily walk of life.

After four months passed, she was reluctantly given permission to return to school one-half day only. Her smile beamed because she knew she could be with her friends and bring a smile to their faces and comfort them throughout the daily stress of being a teenager. Knowing my granddaughter had a heart for the Lord and for others, she was a living example of Jesus and the way He was willing to comfort other people. She longed to get back to her friends—to hear their stories, to share in their disappointments, to encourage the depressed, to laugh at the fun times, to share in their grief, and to rejoice in their accomplishments. My granddaughter longed to see everyone else around her happy and comforted even if she was not happy or needed comfort herself.

So she headed off to school with hair tied back in a ponytail hoping it would go unnoticed by her friends that her thick, sandy-blond hair thinned out to almost nothing. She gained approximately twenty pounds from the high dose of steroids needed in order to keep her kidneys functioning. With very little energy, she was determined to make it through the morning classes so she could be with friends. She took the sly jokes, the remarks about being fat-faced, the negative comments of how she was not a pretty girl any longer, but she never missed an opportunity to come alongside her friends and encourage and compliment them. The school year came to an end, and she was so excited she would be entering into high school the next fall.

The summer months passed quickly. My granddaughter found comfort in hearing her medical specialists tell her she was doing well and improving. Kidney functions improved slightly. The chemo treatments were finished. Steroid intake would be lowered, and the entire family was excited. She would always ask people to pray for her to be healed. Throughout the summer, she shared many of her long-term goals and dreams with me. She would ask me if I thought she would be able to live a normal life ever again. She wondered if she would ever get her thick hair back…if she would even live to grow up and get through college and marry and have a family. She dreamed of being a counselor and being involved in the lives of other people and helping them find comfort and peace. She wanted to go on mission trips to orphanages and just love on the babies and children who did not have the comfort of parents.

We enjoyed a couple of family trips together throughout the summer. Now at fourteen years old, she started her freshman year in high school. She was thrilled to be starting into the next chapter in her life. She began taking drivers training class and was already picking out her first car. In October, she started anticipating the excitement of Christmas and the family times together. She always loved Thanksgiving and Christmas and looked forward to snow in the winter.

On November 24, just three days before Thanksgiving, she was rushed to the emergency room because she was having horrible pain in her legs. Three hours later while being airlifted to Brenner's Children's Hospital in Winston Salem, North Carolina, her heart stopped, and we lost our first grandchild. I needed comfort, and I needed to comfort my daughter and my other three grandchildren. I was completely numb and did not know how I would ever get through it. How do you hold it all together when everyone else needs you to be strong? I was weak. I was helpless. I found myself in a position where I could not even help myself let alone others.

Through the days of tears and suffering, I cried out to God for comfort. Some days I felt abandoned by God. I felt like nothing else mattered any longer, and I would often wonder how I could possibly go on. I was angry, in pain, devastated emotionally, and completely wiped out physically. Even though I had many other family members, I felt lonely without my granddaughter. I had a long list of questions for God, and the heaviness of this loss pinned me down. Would this season of my life ever pass? Could I overcome this time of depression and despair?

I sought the Lord, and He heard my cries. I claimed many promises from the Word of God. I knew God loved me, and He would see me through even when I did not feel it. I knew the Lord understood the pain and grief I was experiencing, and I had to find strength, comfort, and hope from God's Word. God is faithful and can be trusted with the circumstances I faced in life so I had to trust Him. I had to find a way to pursue Him. I knew I had to worship and praise the Lord right through all the grief I was experiencing. I often thought how the Haitian Christians were in hot pursuit of God regardless of their situation, and I knew it was my only way to find comfort. If I could not experience comfort myself, how would I help comfort my daughter who just lost her child and my grandchildren who just lost their sister?

Little by little I made progress and was able to offer encouragement to others. I found that the more I worshipped and praised God, the more I felt His presence and was able to work through this time of grief. Worshipping and praising God in the midst of the storm can be difficult, but it must be done. It is now seven months later, and although I hurt like it was yesterday, I am able to focus on the goodness of God's character. I have been blessed with a church family who ministered to me through this time of crisis. I daily look to see where God is and where He is working in my time of grief. I am able to feel his unwavering love throughout this storm in my life and find comfort in His arms.

Praise be to the God and Father of our Lord Jesus Christ, the Father of compassion and the God of all comfort who comforts us in all our troubles, so that we can comfort those in any trouble with the comfort we ourselves receive from God.[2]

May your unfailing love be my comfort, according to your promise to your servant.[3]

Study Questions

1. Do you truly live well aware that no one else but God can protect you and comfort you from the pitfalls and snares of life?

2. Do you use other things as a substitute that bring you a false sense of security?

3. Do you truly believe He is the only thing you need? Do you call on God for comfort when you need it?

4. Do you start each day making God your Lord, master, and owner? If so, how?

5. Do you recognize God's presence at all times regardless of the various circumstances you are in or emotions you may be experiencing?

6. Do you acknowledge Jesus is yours personally?

7. Is God the shepherd over your life? Do you listen to His voice?

8. How do you overcome times of depression and despair?

13

Security in the Father's House

Voodoo is the dominant religion in Haiti. In 2003 the president of Haiti announced, "Haiti makes voodoo official." Many of the practices and descriptions of this religion sound like superstition, but it is the only religion many of the Haitians living in the remote regions have heard. Many Haitian leaders and government officials endorse the voodoo religion and take it very seriously. Within the country of Haiti, poverty holds a powerful grip on the lives of most people and survival becomes a daily struggle. In the voodoo religion, many different spirits are believed to guide a person throughout his entire life, helping him through the daily struggles. As bad as life seems to the Haitians, they think it would be much worse if they did not believe in the spirits. Spirits are in total control and direct every aspect of their daily lives. The spirits are believed to determine each and every thing that happens in life, and worshippers accept all things have a direct purpose. Nothing happens by chance or coincidence in the life of a voodoo believer.

The Haitian voodoo religion teaches one powerful deity known as Bondieu. He is believed to reign over all the spirits and all of life throughout the entire universe. Voodoo worshippers believe that after death their souls remain to guide other family members. The souls of the dead are considered a major group of the spirits. There are also two additional groups of spirits known as loa spirits controlling the things of nature and the mysterious spirits called the twins. The twins represent contradictory forces like good and evil, rich and poor, healthy and ill, life or death. The more honor given to the spirits, the more likely the worshipper is to receive the better side of the contradicting forces. This belief leaves voodoo worshippers to think they deserve the worst side of the contradicting forces if they do not worship the spirits enough.

Voodoo worshippers honor and take care of the spirits because they believe the spirits depend on them for nourishment. To nourish the spirits, the worshippers sacrifice animals, and they believe they are transferring the spirit of the animal to the spirit itself and give it even more power and control. This process is done by holding a ceremony and honoring the Bondieu and the spirits. Groups gather and worship accompanied by drums and dancing. Individual households nourish the spirits of deceased family members by setting up a table, burning candles, and bringing food and drink and other items that would please the deceased family member. During the ceremony, some worshippers are considered to be possessed by a loa spirit. The loa spirit will give prophetic word to the assembled group, direct cures for some, and offer advice to others in the group through the person possessed by the spirit. The loa is in full control of the worshipper's body and generally causes the body to dance in an uncontrollable manner. Once the individual is completely exhausted from dancing, the body is released by the loa.

Believers possess a great amount of power that is quite dangerous in one group called Petro Voodoo. This group practices black magic and sorcery. The most common group in Haiti is Rada. This group believes that when the spirits are angry, they will inflict illness on people. Many diseases and unsanitary conditions already exist. Diseases are prevalent in Haiti, and Rada followers perform healing ceremonies attempting to heal through casting spells or giving some form of herbal remedy. Voodoo is a culture attempting to meet all spiritual and material needs of the people. The leaders believe they have power to do what one wishes, to make others give to increase their wealth, make others perform actions against their will, or harm others without suffering any consequences. The women are mistreated in many ways because men see themselves as superior to women. Women are often physically and emotionally abused.

Many Christian beliefs and traditions are incorporated into the flexible voodoo religion so it becomes confusing to many Haitians. They long for a sense of security. They long for someone they can trust and have their best interest at heart. With voodoo being a common way of life, many Haitians attempt to find security in the spirits and long to join in helping the future generations upon their death. They rely on Bondieu and spirits to take care of their needs from one day to the next while living and for all eternity. I could not help but wonder why they were so poor and hungry and not many of their needs met if the Bondieu was taking care of their daily needs. They live in a false sense of security and need to hear how they can find security in Christ Jesus. When I left Haiti, my prayer for the Haitians became the words found in Luke 10:2, "The harvest is plentiful, but the workers are few. Ask the Lord of the harvest, therefore, to send out workers into his harvest field."

As I watched and listened to the voodoo priest and some of his followers screaming in the street, cursing the Christians and missionaries and trying to cast spells on them, I noticed it had very little effect on the Haitian Christians. If the followers of voodoo were so sure their god was the only god and he would take care of all their needs, I wondered why they were so concerned about getting the men and women of God discouraged and were trying to cast spells on them. What did they have to worry about? Would their god not protect them and take care of them like they believed? No doubt the Christians stood firm on promises in the Word of God. They no doubt knew who they were in Christ Jesus and felt safe and secure.

> What, then, shall we say in response to these things? If God is for us, who can be against us? He who did not spare his own Son, but gave Him up for us all—how will he not also, along with Him, graciously give us all things?[1]

The Christians knew God was for them, and if He promised to give them all things, protection was one of those things. "Who shall separate us from the love of Christ? Shall trouble or hardship or persecution or famine or nakedness or danger or sword?"[2] They were confident no thing or no person had power to take them away from God and the love He had for them. I am sure they wanted to waiver in their faith at times when experiencing hardships like they had to face every day, while being persecuted and mocked by the voodoo worshippers, experiencing famine and nakedness, and living in danger of being robbed of what little they had. "In all these things we are more than conquerors through him who loved us."[3] Even if they lost every material possession they had, the Christians stood firm and believed no one could snatch them out of the hand of God. Knowing Christ as Savior brought them into a relationship with the Father guaranteeing eternal security and protection until He was ready to take them home. They were "convinced that neither death nor life, neither angels nor demons, neither the present nor the future, nor any powers, neither height nor depth, nor anything else in all creation, will be able to separate us from the love of God that is in Christ Jesus our Lord."[4] I knew they had to find security in believing these verses to be true.

Once we are adopted as His children, we too can feel secure living in His house. "For our citizenship is in heaven, from which also we eagerly wait for a Savior, the Lord Jesus Christ."[5] If we know who we are in Christ, we can feel safe and secure. They know and so can we that God has everything in control, and all we need to do is eagerly wait. The security you can find living in the Father's house is unending.

Military men are trained to lead by example, to put the strongest and most trained forces up front. The colonel wants those who are strongest, well trained, and accurate in shooting in the front line leading the others into battle. As the battle unfolds in the days ahead, the strong believers must lead by example, be strong and courageous, be willing to stand on the front line and know that all their strength is found in the Lord. We must be willing to stand on the front line for what we believe, knowing that our security will be found in the Heavenly Father and we will live in His house forever and ever.

Hebrews 13:6 says, "So that we confidently say, the Lord is my Helper, I will not be afraid. What will man do to me?" With a firm foundation in the Lord, you can have the same security I saw in the Haitian Christians. A strong foundation brings perfect security, and security brings perfect peace and protection. Satan always tries to bring you down by using others to make you feel insecure so it is important to remember who you are in the Lord. You are an heir to His kingdom as a child of the living God. We often take our eyes off God and forget that the Lord's eyes are always on us. When we feel insecure and think we are facing this world alone, we need to think again. Focus your gaze on the Father who is standing right there with you and find your comfort in Jesus who will be all the security you need.

Needing to feel secure is a feeling we all desire. We fight with giving up control for fear we will lose our security. Our focus needs to be redirected on making God our security. We need to cry out, "Like a swallow, like a crane, so I twitter; I moan like a dove; My eyes look wistfully to the heights; O Lord, I am oppressed, be my security."[6] If you let the closeness of God be your security, you will find a renewed freedom to move forward in your relationship with the Heavenly Father. Trusting God has your best interest in mind; it is much easier to allow Him to be in control of your life. If God becomes your security, you will have nothing to fear. It will not be difficult to relinquish all demands for God to do what you want to do on your own.

You can experience God as your security. "He provides them with security, and they are supported."[7] When the Spirit of God becomes your security, control is no longer needed. We go through life looking for power and control and block the security the Heavenly Father wants to provide for us. You are designed to experience God, so let go and allow Him to be your security. Stop looking for security in earthly things instead of God.

He who dwells in the shelter of the Most High will abide in the shadow of the Almighty. I will say to the Lord, My refuge and my fortress, my God, in whom I trust! For it is He who delivers you from the snare of the trapper and from the deadly pestilence. He will cover you with His pinions, and under His wings you may seek refuge; His faithfulness is a shield and bulwark.[8]

This is a promise for security beyond what most Christians even begin to experience.

Count it pure joy to know that no matter what comes your way, your security is found in the Lord. Security in the Lord is found when you know that you completely trust in the Lord and that He will work all things out according to His will for your life. We are all designed with a longing to rest in the presence of God but often find security in earthly things instead. We cannot look to another human to meet our need for security. People cannot replace Jesus! Set the Lord continually before you; keep Him at your right hand and do not be shaken. Let your heart be glad, rejoice, and let your flesh dwell securely in the Father's arms.[9]

Study Questions

1. Are you in control of your life or have you relinquished control to God? If you are still in control, does being in control provide you security?

2. Do you base your worth on who God says you are or on what you do?

3. Watching the Haitian Christians, I could see they were resting in the arms of God and finding security even in their difficulties. Why do you think people hang on to pain and hurt rather than looking for the good in troubles and finding security trusting in God?

4. Do you really receive God's love for you? Do you know you have eternal life with God? Are you hanging onto the promise in John 10:28–29 and believe nothing can snatch you from the hand of God?

5. I am amazed when I reflect on how much security Jesus had in His Father. He definitely found security in knowing He was fulfilling the will of His Father. He looked to His Father for direction and was obedient even to the point of death on the cross. He knew His eternity was secure by His Father's side. Are you fully obedient to God-secure in knowing His way is best? Are you secure knowing your destiny is eternity with Him in heaven?

14

Residency in the Father's House

Haitian Christians demonstrated God's love to those around them, not just with words but also in deed. They were doers of the Word and not merely hearers who deceive themselves. In James 1, James goes on to say that if anyone is a hearer of the word and not a doer, he is like a man who looks at his natural face in a mirror, and once he sees himself and goes away from the mirror, he immediately forgets what kind of person he is.[1] It is easy to look at yourself and think you are doing your part and deceive yourself. But the real test is to look at yourself the same way Jesus looks at you. Are you feeding the poor, casting our demons, helping the captive find freedom, healing the sick, sharing the good news of Christ Jesus, and loving others more than you love yourself?

Many Christians are deceived. We live in a time when the world must die as we know it today—a time when Christians need to start acting like they live in the Father's house the way God laid out in the Bible. We live in a time when people around the world need to fall on their faces before God and drastically change, questioning their traditions and beliefs instead of accepting them from what they heard or were taught. Rather than fitting into the communities in which we live, we need to exhibit Christianity and influence our communities. We have daily chores to do if we truly live in the Father's house, and we need to do our part to get the house in order.

God's will becomes a way of life if you are living in the kingdom of God. Living in the kingdom is available to anyone willing to surrender his will to align with God's will. When your will, mind, and body are made available to God as instruments in His hands, then you are living in the kingdom of God—residing in His house. Revelation 1:5b–6, "To him who loves us and has freed us from our sins by his blood, and has made us to be a kingdom and priests to serve his God and Father." When your will unites with His will, you become connected to the very life and power of God. "For the kingdom of God is not a matter of talk but of power."[2] Carnal habits are hard to break, and they are our greatest hindrance to kingdom living. We are constantly bombarded with distractions preoccupying us with self or others causing us to withdraw from complete submission to the will of God. Don't settle for substitutes. Reside in His kingdom. Take up residency in the Father's house.

If you read chapter 1 of Haggai, you read of the historical occasion where the remnant that had returned from captivity became selfishly caught up in their own affairs. They became more concerned about the beauty and condition of their own dwellings rather than in rebuilding the Lord's house. God's house had remained in ruins and yet the people were living in the comfort of their own homes. God had withheld natural blessings from the people because of the lack of concern for the temple. The Lord questions the people, wondering if it is time for them to dwell in their own houses, to keep storing up possessions, and to allow the temple to continue to remain in ruins. I think this is a question God wants to ask us today. Are we building up so many personal possessions and larger and better structures for ourselves? Do we have little or no concern about building His house?

The story continues, and God challenges with a command: "Give careful thought to your ways!"[3] Obviously, He was not too pleased with the lifestyle He was seeing, and He wanted the people to seriously think and examine themselves. He wanted them to judge for themselves whether or not they were doing the right things. Again, I think the Lord is asking individuals the same question today. He wants us to give careful thought to our lifestyles and see if they are pleasing Him.

In My Father's House

The Lord gave orders for the remnant to go up the mountain and bring down timber to build the house of the Lord so He could be pleased and be honored in it. He wanted them to see that while each of them as individuals was busy with his own house—God's house remained in ruins. To all of you who are reading this book, The Lord God Almighty is calling forth a remnant to *go* and build the temple. He is looking for individuals who are not too busy building wealth and possessions for themselves and who will invest in the lives of others and help rebuild the temple: the house of the Lord. If you wonder why God is blowing everything you have away, it may be because His house remains in ruins. If you find yourself in this position, if you feel you are in a drought, if you feel you don't have enough of what the world and men produce through the labor of their hands—my friend, it is time to change. If your belief is that God wants to work in and through you, your hands and resources are His. Use it, give it to Him, and *help rebuild* the temple.

God was not happy back then with the people's choices, and He is not happy with the world today. Things were not working out for them, and things are not working out for many people around the world today. He was and still is in control, and He wants people to put their trust in Him. He wants you to give "careful thought to your ways." He wants your focus to change. He wants you to be in His plan, doing His will and rebuilding the Father's House so He can find pleasure in it and be honored.

> All the remnant of the people obeyed the voice of the lord their God…and the people showed reverence for the Lord. Then Haggai, the messenger of the lord, spoke by the commission of the Lord to the people saying, 'I am with you,' declares the Lord.[4]

If your house is not in order and you desire to live in the Father's house, you must be restored to the Father if you are not living like one of His children. Far too many Christians have drifted away from closeness with the Father and need to be restored. God wants the days of our future to be greater than the days of our past. He wants to give you a life and give it to you more abundantly. "The thief comes only to steal and kill and destroy; I came that they may have life, and have it abundantly."[5] These are the words of Jesus Himself. Satan is the thief. So if you are not living an abundant life, know that God wants to give you a new hope through divine forgiveness and reconciliation. You can be delivered from the past and restored to an intimate relationship with Him. He wants the Holy Spirit to work within you and give you the power you need to live a victorious Christian life. Christ wants to be exalted in your body.

Others reading this book may have never even become a child of the King. You may have never accepted Jesus Christ as your personal Savior. This would be a good time to make a commitment to live for Jesus and take up residency in the Father's house. We are all born sinners, and in Romans, we are told,

> That if you confess with your mouth Jesus *as* Lord, and believe in your heart that God raised Him from the dead, you will be saved; for with the heart a person believes, resulting in righteousness, and with the mouth he confesses, resulting in salvation.[6]

The very next verse gets even more encouraging. The Scripture says, "Whoever believes in Him will not be disappointed."[7] Wow! What a beautiful promise. If He promises us we will not be disappointed, why not believe in Him and take up residency in His house?

As you gain a more intimate relationship with the Father (living in *His* house), you will also gain insight to know His plans to move forward in your life for Him. In the book, I wrote, "Lost in the Wilderness," I talked about the Father's desire to restore the Father-child relationship. Although I did not like losing my earthly father, God gave me grace to get through it. Through this loss, I matured spiritually, and I gained the desire to restore and continue to build an intimate relationship with the Father. Then I returned home to live in the Father's house. During this time, I obtained a higher level of perseverance and started seeing a brighter hope for my future.

> Therefore, having been justified by faith, we have peace with God through our Lord Jesus Christ, through whom also we have obtained our introduction by faith into this grace in which we stand; and we exult in hope of the glory of God. And not only this, but we also exult in our tribulations, knowing that tribulation brings about perseverance; and perseverance, proven character; and proven character, hope; and hope does not disappoint, because the love of God has been poured out within our hearts through the Holy Spirit who was given to us.[8]

Once you are a child of the Heavenly Father, have an intimate relationship with Him and live in His house under His authority, you begin to see your faith grow. The love of God will be poured out in your heart and your character will change. You will gain a new joy—a greater joy than you have ever known if you reside in the Father's house. He will do just what it says in Psalms 30; He will turn your mourning into dancing and loosen your sackcloth and gird you with gladness.[9]

When I was in Haiti, we would teach the women early in the morning. The women who came for Bible teaching at 6:00 a.m. were looking for nourishment to grow. They came for a fresh renewal of heart and mind—eager for the Holy Spirit to renew and regenerate them. They were looking to reside in the kingdom of God every day of their lives right here on earth in the little village of Belami. "He saved us, not on the basis of deeds which we have done in righteousness, but according to His mercy, by the washing of regeneration and renewing by the Holy Spirit."[10] The women came early, and when they left to go about their daily chores, the Holy Spirit had given them a new strength to move forward. The early morning teaching gave them the opportunity to sit still and quietly rest before the Lord. "In repentance and rest you will be saved, in quietness and trust is your strength."[11]

With all that these women had to endure on a daily basis, gardening, preparing food, carrying water for miles, handwashing clothes (just a few of the daily chores) in the extreme heat, they needed all the strength and refreshing the Lord had to offer. With the hard life the Haitian women live, I could only pray the favor of the Lord would fall upon them. I hoped they could find pleasure and delight in pleasing God and that God could look at them and be so pleased that His favor would rest upon them. With His favor, they could accomplish things on earth and have access to places in the heavenly realm they had not previously been.

"You have granted me life and loving-kindness; and Your care has preserved my spirit."[12] I wanted God to preserve these women as they lived their lives here on earth until they entered the Father's house for eternity. It wasn't just the women, but many men and children as well. They were truly chasing after God. They were after a fresh presence of the Almighty God every day. Whether in or out of church, they were in His presence as they went about their everyday lives. If you want to pursue a relationship and really *know* Him, you must do more than just study God's Word. You have to know where He is now and what He is doing now. Too many Christians are content studying where God has been throughout history instead of running hard and in hot pursuit of Him today. I find myself like some of the Haitian Christians I witnessed—seeking God with all my heart until I find revelation and see His existence in the present time. We all need present truth from the Heavenly Father. We should all long for encounters with God. Back when I was a bench-warming Christian, I knew about God and knew a lot of the Bible stories. But once I started running after God, He could speak to me and my understanding was much clearer. His voice would speak to me at night through dreams and at moments throughout the day. My Heavenly Father was not concerned about how much I knew from merely reading. His concern was how well I intimately knew him. This is the same concern He has for each of His children. He longs for a deep, close relationship with each child.

When I lost my earthly father, the Heavenly Father wanted my full attention. I was empty inside without my father, and I had to refocus my attention on getting to know the Heavenly Father the way I should. Church became a customary practice, but I was still empty. I needed a deeper connection with the Father. I had to work on building my relationship with Him to know all He was offering me. I had to want a Father/daughter relationship with Him. I was ready to wait on Him to empower me and stop trying to do so much in my own power. I was going to wait on the Lord to renew my strength.[13]

God wants to repossess the church. He wants to renew our strength and pour out His Spirit on anyone hungry enough to want it. If you are filled with the Spirit until it is pouring out to others, then you are effective in building the kingdom, and it does not have to be in any particular building or organization. Door-to-door, small home groups, and one-on-one ministry worked in Bible days and it still works today. It is the excitement of individuals that will really spread the Word of God. We do not have to keep trying to make things happen. We merely have to hunger and thirst for the Spirit to fill us until we are overflowing. Then things will happen.

People believe it is mainly the pastor's role to witness, visit, and lead people to Christ to expand the growth of the church. While a pastor may be called to lead, preach, and teach a congregation, it is the responsibility of each person to rub off on another to build the kingdom. As the pastor disciples us, we need to disciple others. Once we invest in the lives of others on a more personal level, then they are more apt to become excited about being involved in a corporate level. Many people feel unaccepted and intimidated by large crowds and find it much easier to feel accepted in a smaller group. It is much easier to see and meet the needs of individuals when dealing with a smaller group or an individual versus in a large group or organization. I have heard far too many people say they felt lost in the shuffle in a large organization. They simply feel overlooked. I think God is more pleased when we are focused on individuals rather than on buildings and what we can accomplish within the walls of the buildings.

When doing work in Haiti, the amount of fellowship that went on in individual homes, outside in the streets, or simply from house to house was very effective. Many village areas do not even have a church site, but the church had strong believers in Christ Jesus spreading the Word of God. They had people proclaiming as they went, saying, "Repent, for the kingdom of heaven is at hand."[14]

If your life is encumbered with sin, it is time to fall on your face before God and repent. To truly live in the Father's house, you have to invest time to really *know* God. You have to make a conscious decision that you will do whatever it takes because you must have Him. You cannot worry about the cost. Whatever the cost may be, it will not be too much to pay.

Wherever I travel, I notice church buildings. My husband and personal photographer knows to take photos of them for me. He is aware of my interest in the various designs, sizes, styles, and expenses put into the buildings. While some show amazing detail in architectural design, others have expensive glass-stained windows and elaborate interiors with all the necessary amenities. Still other buildings are just simple structures for people to come into the house of the Lord. I am not saying there is anything wrong with the design or expense of the church building itself, but I do feel if the hearts of those who gather in the Father's house belong to God, if they are adopted children into the kingdom of God, the Father is pleased. When too much emphasis is placed on the structure instead of the relationship with God, the purpose of the building is overlooked. We should be prepared to praise and worship God, receive instruction, celebrate, teach, serve one another, show love, find joy and peace as we strive for an even deeper, intimate relationship with the Father. After all, we are the temple of God! "The kingdom of God is not coming with signs to be observed, nor will people say, 'Look here it is,' or 'Look there it is,' For behold the kingdom of God is in your midst."[15]

In the Father's house, you have a peace that surpasses all understanding—it is beyond our comprehension. In the Father's house, there are lots of hugs, a deep feeling of love and comfort, for security as you rest nestled in the Father's arms. It is a place where you go to find rest and just relax with daddy. His house is a home where acceptance abounds—no judgment, no condemnation, and no criticism. All is done with proper correction and teaching along with a heart of concern. The Father blesses those who live in His house and makes provision for the children. He expects His children to succeed and embrace His promises. While the Father expects us to be obedient, He allows room for failure and mistakes so we can learn. In His house, we are to share all we have and not be greedy, remembering others always come first. The Father will tuck you in at night with security beyond what a security system has to offer. He is monitoring your safety every minute and has His own built-in alarming sounds.

John 16:23 says that in the Father's house, you can ask for anything you want. He will provide if it is for the right motives according to His will. The Father wants your joy to be complete. He knows in this world you will have trouble, but He wants you to take heart and know He has overcome the world. We have a place with God. Exodus 33:21 "Then the Lord said, 'there is a place near me where you may stand on a rock.'" Just like the Lord spoke to Moses, we too can stand on the rock if we desire to do so. Although we cannot see His face, we can be as close to Him as we desire. We can be near Him! We can take up residency in His house and begin living in the kingdom now!

Study Questions

1. Are you demonstrating God's love in such a way that others see Christ in you or are you deceiving yourself?

2. Is the lifestyle you are living pleasing to God? Will you give careful thought to your ways?

3. Will you be obedient to the Lord and change what is displeasing to Him? It will be impossible for you to do your part rebuilding the Father's house until you take the first step and stop worrying about building up self.

4. Are you intentionally submitting your life to the will of God?

5. Do you need to rethink the way you live? Change your life and believe the Word of God? Will you allow God to invade your life and change you right now?

6. Do you feel like your life is in a rut? Do you feel like you are planting much but have no harvest? Do you need to reevaluate what you are planting? Are you planting seeds for a great harvest or seeds of discord, strife, hatred, and bitterness?

7. Do you need to clothe yourself with a robe of righteousness or do you put on clothes and still feel cold?

Notes

Chapter 2: A Vision Birthed

1. Jer. 29:11 (NIV).
2. John 10:10 (NASB).
3. Matt. 6:24 (NASB).
4. Phil. 3:13–14 (NASB).
5. Phil. 1:20 (NIV).

Chapter 3: Being a Servant in the Father's House

1. Luke 17:7–10 (NIV).
2. Philippians 2:5–7 (NIV).
3. Eph. 6:7 (NIV).
4. John 6:5b (NASB).
5. Prov. 22:9 (NASB).
6. Matt. 20:27–28 (NASB).
7. 1 Sam. 3:10 (NASB).
8. 1 Sam. 12:20 (NASB).
9. Josh. 24:15 (NASB).
10. James 1:14–16 (NIV).

Chapter 4: Room in the Father's House

1. Luke 19:1–10 (NIV).
2. Luke 2:8–20 (NIV).
3. John 14:2 (NASB).
4. John 14:18 (NASB).
5. Phil. 3:20 (NASB).
6. Matt. 6:19–21 (NIV).

7. 2 Cor. 5:1 (NASB).
8. Heb. 11:10 (NASB).

Chapter 5: Peace in the Father's House

1. Isa. 26:3 (NASB).
2. Ps. 34:14 (NIV).
3. Ps. 29:11 (NIV).
4. Eph. 2:14 (NASB).
5. Ps. 4:8 (NASB).
6. Exod. 3:6 (NASB).
7. Exod. 4:10 (NASB).
8. Exod. 4:11–12 (NASB).
9. Luke 1:79 (NIV).

Chapter 6: Celebration in The Father's House

1. Acts 16: 22–34 (NIV).
2. James 2:14–17 (NIV).
3. James 2:8 (NIV).
4. Mark 8:22–25 (NIV).
5. Galatians 5:1 (NASB).
6. Isaiah 61:1 (NASB).

Chapter 7: Love in the Father's House

1. Luke 21:1–4 (NIV).
2. 1 Pet. 1:22 (NASB).
3. John 15:12 (NASB).
4. 1 Cor. 10:31 (NASB).
5. James 2:8 (NASB).
6. Rom. 13:8 (NASB).
7. Gal. 5:13–14 (NASB).

Chapter 8: Intimacy in the Father's House

1. 2 Cor. 6:18 (NIV),
2. Gal. 4:4–7 (NIV).
3. Luke 5:16 (NASB).
4. Eph. 6:18 (NASB).
5. James 4:8 (NIV).
6. 1 Cor. 1:9 (NASB).

Chapter 9: Joy in the Father's House

1. John 10:10 (NASB).
2. Neh. 8:10b (NASB).
3. Ps. 37:4 (NASB).
4. Rom. 14:17 (NASB).
5. Phil. 3:7–9 (NASB).
6. Ps. 45:7 (NIV).
7. John 15:10–11 (NASB).
8. John Piper, True Christianity: Inexpressible Joy in the Invisible God
9. 1 Pet. 1:8 (NIV).
10. Heb. 11:25 (NIV).

Chapter 10: Instruction in the Father's House

1. 2 Tim. 3:16–17 (NASB).
2. Mal. 3:6 (NASB).
3. Matt. 5, 9, 13, 18, 24 and 25 (Good chapters in reference to instructions for Christian living).
4. Matt. 22:37 (NASB).
5. Matt. 22:39 (NASB).
6. Deut. 5:29 (NIV).
7. Matt. 4:4 (NASB).
8. John 15:19 (NIV).
9. John 3:3 (NASB).
10. John 3:5–6 (NIV).

Chapter 11: Praise and Worship in the Father's House

1. Isa. 2:3 (NASB).
2. Ps. 28:2 (NIV).
3. Ps. 134:2 (NIV).
4. Ps. 141:2 (NIV).
5. Ps. 143:6 (NASB).
6. Ps. 47:1, 6–7 (NASB).
7. John 4:23–24 (NASB).
8. James 1:12 (NASB).
9. John 4:24 (NIV).
10. Rom. 12:1–2 (NIV).

Chapter 12: Comfort in the Father's House

1. Ps. 23 (NASB).
2. 2 Cor. 1:3–4 (NIV).
3. Ps. 119:76 (NIV).

Chapter 13: Security in the Father's House

1. Rom. 8:31–32 (NIV).
2. Rom. 8:35 (NIV).
3. Rom. 8:37 (NIV).
4. Rom. 8:38–39 (NIV).
5. Phil. 3:20 (NASB).
6. Isa. 38:14 (NASB).
7. Job 24:23a (NASB).
8. Ps. 91:1–4 (NASB).
9. Ps. 16:8–9 (NASB).

Chapter 14. Residency in the Father's House

1. James 1:22–25 (NIV).
2. 1 Cor. 4:20 (NIV).
3. Hag. 1:5 (NIV).
4. Hag. 1:12–14 (NASB).

5. John 10:10 (NASB).
6. Rom. 10:9–10 (NIV).
7. Rom. 10:11 (NASB).
8. Rom. 5:1–5 (NASB).
9. Ps. 30:11 (NASB).
10. Tit. 3:5 (NASB).
11. Isa. 30:15 (NASB).
12. Job 10:12 (NASB).
13. Isa. 40:31a (NIV).
14. Matt. 3:2 (NASB).
15. Luke 17:20–21 (NASB).

CPSIA information can be obtained
at www.ICGtesting.com
Printed in the USA
FFOW05n0936061016